Getting Bigger
by Growing Smaller

A New Growth Model for Corporate America

FT Prentice Hall
FINANCIAL TIMES

In an increasingly competitive world, it is quality
of thinking that gives an edge—an idea that opens new
doors, a technique that solves a problem, or an insight
that simply helps make sense of it all.

We work with leading authors in the various arenas
of business and finance to bring cutting-edge thinking
and best learning practice to a global market.

It is our goal to create world-class print publications
and electronic products that give readers
knowledge and understanding which can then be
applied, whether studying or at work.

To find out more about our business
products, you can visit us at www.ft-ph.com

Pearson
Education

Getting Bigger
by Growing Smaller

A New Growth Model for Corporate America

Joel M. Shulman
Thomas T. Stallkamp

An Imprint of PEARSON EDUCATION

Upper Saddle River, NJ • New York • London • San Francisco • Toronto • Sydney
Tokyo • Singapore • Hong Kong • Cape Town • Madrid
Paris • Milan • Munich • Amsterdam

www.ft-ph.com

Library of Congress Cataloging-in-Publication Data

A CIP catalog record for this book can be obtained from the Library of Congress

Editorial/Production Supervision: Wil Mara
Cover Design Director: Jerry Votta
Cover Design: Talar Boorujy
Art Director: Gail Cocker-Bogusz
Interior Design: Meg VanArsdale
Manufacturing Manager: Alexis R. Heydt-Long
Executive Editor: Jim Boyd
Editorial Assistant: Linda Ramagnano
Marketing Manager: John Pierce

© 2004 Pearson Education, Inc.
Publishing as Financial Times Prentice Hall
Upper Saddle River, New Jersey 07458

Financial Times Prentice Hall books are widely used by corporations and government agencies for training, marketing, and resale.

For information regarding corporate and government builk discounts, please contact: Corporate and Government Sales, 1-800-382-3419, or corpsales@pearsontechgroup.com.

Printed in the United States of America

First Printing

ISBN 0-13-008422-0

Pearson Education Ltd.
Pearson Education Australia Pty., Limited
Pearson Education Singapore, Pte. Ltd.
Pearson Education North Asia Ltd.
Pearson Education Canada, Ltd.
Pearson Educación de Mexico, S.A. de C.V.
Pearson Education—Japan
Pearson Education Malaysia, Pte. Ltd.

FINANCIAL TIMES PRENTICE HALL BOOKS

For more information, please go to www.ft-ph.com

Business and Technology

Sarv Devaraj and Rajiv Kohli
The IT Payoff: Measuring the Business Value of Information Technology Investments

Nicholas D. Evans
Business Innovation and Disruptive Technology: Harnessing the Power of Breakthrough Technology…for Competitive Advantage

Nicholas D. Evans
Consumer Gadgets: 50 Ways to Have Fun and Simplify Your Life with Today's Technology…and Tomorrow's

Faisal Hoque
The Alignment Effect: How to Get Real Business Value Out of Technology

Economics

David Dranove
What's Your Life Worth? Health Care Rationing…Who Lives? Who Dies? Who Decides?

John C. Edmunds
Brave New Wealthy World: Winning the Struggle for World Prosperity

Jonathan Wight
Saving Adam Smith: A Tale of Wealth, Transformation, and Virtue

Entrepreneurship

Oren Fuerst and Uri Geiger
From Concept to Wall Street: A Complete Guide to Entrepreneurship and Venture Capital

David Gladstone and Laura Gladstone
Venture Capital Handbook: An Entrepreneur's Guide to Raising Venture Capital, Revised and Updated

Thomas K. McKnight
Will It Fly? How to Know if Your New Business Idea Has Wings… Before You Take the Leap

Erica Orloff and Kathy Levinson, Ph.D.
The 60-Second Commute: A Guide to Your 24/7 Home Office Life

Jeff Saperstein and Daniel Rouach
Creating Regional Wealth in the Innovation Economy: Models, Perspectives, and Best Practices

Stephen Spinelli, Jr., Robert M. Rosenberg, and Sue Birley
Franchising: Pathway to Wealth Creation

Executive Skills

Cyndi Maxey and Jill Bremer
It's Your Move: Dealing Yourself the Best Cards in Life and Work

Finance

Aswath Damodaran
The Dark Side of Valuation: Valuing Old Tech, New Tech, and New Economy Companies

Kenneth R. Ferris and Barbara S. Pécherot Petitt
Valuation: Avoiding the Winner's Curse

International Business

Peter Marber
Money Changes Everything: How Global Prosperity Is Reshaping Our Needs, Values, and Lifestyles

Fernando Robles, Françoise Simon, and Jerry Haar
Winning Strategies for the New Latin Markets

Investments

Zvi Bodie and Michael J. Clowes
Worry-Free Investing: A Safe Approach to Achieving Your Lifetime Goals

Harry Domash
Fire Your Stock Analyst! Analyzing Stocks on Your Own

David Gladstone and Laura Gladstone
Venture Capital Investing: The Complete Handbook for Investing in Businesses for Outstanding Profits

D. Quinn Mills
Buy, Lie, and Sell High: How Investors Lost Out on Enron and the Internet Bubble

D. Quinn Mills
Wheel, Deal, and Steal: Deceptive Accounting, Deceitful CEOs, and Ineffective Reforms

John Nofsinger and Kenneth Kim
Infectious Greed: Restoring Confidence in America's Companies

John R. Nofsinger
Investment Blunders (of the Rich and Famous)…And What You Can Learn from Them

John R. Nofsinger
Investment Madness: How Psychology Affects Your Investing…And What to Do About It

H. David Sherman, S. David Young, and Harris Collingwood
Profits You Can Trust: Spotting & Surviving Accounting Landmines

Leadership

Jim Despain and Jane Bodman Converse
And Dignity for All: Unlocking Greatness through Values-Based Leadership

Marshall Goldsmith, Vijay Govindarajan, Beverly Kaye, and Albert A. Vicere
The Many Facets of Leadership

Marshall Goldsmith, Cathy Greenberg, Alastair Robertson, and Maya Hu-Chan
Global Leadership: The Next Generation

Management

Rob Austin and Lee Devin
Artful Making: What Managers Need to Know About How Artists Work

J. Stewart Black and Hal B. Gregersen
Leading Strategic Change: Breaking Through the Brain Barrier

William C. Byham, Audrey B. Smith, and Matthew J. Paese
Grow Your Own Leaders: How to Identify, Develop, and Retain Leadership Talent

David M. Carter and Darren Rovell
On the Ball: What You Can Learn About Business from Sports Leaders

Subir Chowdhury
Organization 21C: Someday All Organizations Will Lead this Way

Ross Dawson
*Living Networks: Leading Your Company, Customers, and Partners
in the Hyper-connected Economy*

Charles J. Fombrun and Cees B.M. Van Riel
Fame and Fortune: How Successful Companies Build Winning Reputations

Amir Hartman
Ruthless Execution: What Business Leaders Do When Their Companies Hit the Wall

Harvey A. Hornstein
*The Haves and the Have Nots: The Abuse of Power and Privilege in the Workplace…
and How to Control It*

Kevin Kennedy and Mary Moore
Going the Distance: Why Some Companies Dominate and Others Fail

Robin Miller
The Online Rules of Successful Companies: The Fool-Proof Guide to Building Profits

Fergus O'Connell
The Competitive Advantage of Common Sense: Using the Power You Already Have

W. Alan Randolph and Barry Z. Posner
*Checkered Flag Projects: 10 Rules for Creating and Managing Projects that Win,
Second Edition*

Stephen P. Robbins
Decide & Conquer: Make Winning Decisions to Take Control of Your Life

Stephen P. Robbins
The Truth About Managing People…And Nothing but the Truth

Contents

3   What's Wrong with the Current System? Compensation without Long-Term Value Creation 37

4   Resistance to Change— Ways to Leverage the Concrete Middle 57

5 Growth Models Need to Change 71

6 A New Growth Model 93

7   Implementing the SEU 125

8   Financing an SEU Venture 141

9 Liquidity versus Liquidation: Cashing Out of the SEU 161

10 Where Do We Go from Here? Jumpstarting the Process of Change 179

Index 209

Acknowledgements

There are a number of people that helped contribute to this book that deserve recognition. Editor Jim Boyd provided enormous support throughout the process along with timely input from production editor Wil Mara, and content reviewer Harris Collingwood. In the early stages, Steven Kursh (Professor from Northeastern), John Grant (affiliated with MIT's entrepreneurship group), Harvard classmate, Dan Schneider all helped develop the formation of this book and a template for future academic courses at Babson College. As part of this formation, Babson's faculty and administration provided support and encouragement for a new Corporate Entrepreneurship track. This group includes: Babson Provost Michael Fetters, Dean Mark Rice, Professor Jeffrey Timmons, Professor William Bygrave, Professor Allan Cohen, Professor Steven Spinelli, Professor Shaker Zahra, Professor Paul Reynolds and Babson College President Brian Barefoot. Distinguished alumni and other Babson personnel also contributed including: Robert Weissman, Arthur Blank, Michael Smith, former Babson President William Glavin and Thomas Krimmel. And, indirect support came from colleagues and former colleagues such as Les Charm and Professor Roberto Bonifaz, whose frequent queries kept motivation high and focus sharp.

Much of the research was conducted at Harvard University in which several faculty members of the Harvard Business School, Law School, and Kennedy School of Government contributed significantly. We mention them separately in the Introduction. Many Babson students provided early research support including: Lesley Edwards, Reddi Rayalu, and Jay Mehta. Carrie Geeck from MSXI also provided terrific assistance along the way.

Periodic inspiration came from several gatherings including: Rockport's Emerson Inn, New Hampshire's Adair Inn and a Goldman Sach's conference room (where the chapter on compensation was developed).

Clearly, one of the most significant factors in developing this book has been the input from coauthor and contributor, Thomas Stallkamp. It has been a great pleasure to collaborate with him these past three years. His brilliant insight drawn from years of experience at large organizations enabled us to address the core issues of corporate growth (at all levels of the organization) and help develop practical solutions to corporate dilemma. He is a class individual, whose well-timed humor, work ethic and support were essential for completing this project. Without his collaboration with the encouragement from his wonderful wife Ann, this would have been just another academic or theoretical treatise.

Finally, I would like to thank my lovely wife Kristen for her steadfast support and encouragement. Her understanding, proof reading and personal sacrifices made this project manageable and her watchful eye over our beautiful children Jared, Alissa, Sari and Janelle were indispensable. To all, my heartfelt thanks.

Joel M. Shulman

Introduction

Corporate leaders today have a difficult task in trying to achieve growth within their large organizations. Global competition has increased, risk capital providers have reduced their investments, and organizational motivations/incentives tend to work against effective long-term growth and survival. Large companies continue to pursue growth, but they tend to focus on "big bets" or major investments/ acquisitions. The rationale for this approach is that only a large investment can make a difference to large, publicly traded organizations. Consequently, senior management tends to spend its time on large strategic projects or acquisitions—not small-scale entrepreneurial initiatives, when exploring growth initiatives. This book suggests that management can do both. In fact, to the extent that management pursues lots of small initiatives (with external parties overseeing the time consuming tasks of deal filtering and analysis), the large organization can leverage its research and development without incurring additional investment. Moreover, pursuing many small, entrepreneurial projects helps diversify the portfolio of risk investments and reduces the risk associated with any major project failing.

This book introduces a new concept referred to as a Strategic Entrepreneurial Unit (SEU). Properly set up and managed, the SEU not only offers many corporations a mechanism for continual renewal, it also alters the structure of corporate incentives, giving senior executives, middle managers, and line employees strong inducement to create lasting corporate value. The model focuses on enhancing the long-term health of the enterprise through strategic affiliations with many small companies. Essentially, the SEU template provides an opportunity for entrepreneurs either internal or external to the large organization, to partner with the big company. This facility creates high potential growth ventures leveraging the brand, intellectual property and infrastructure of the parent without burdening the new SEU venture with the cost structure, corporate culture or politicking of the large company. But this format is not for all companies, and it is not a panacea for poor management, institutional malaise, or an industrial decline.

The concept of the Strategic Entrepreneurial Unit (SEU) emerged from conversations with Corporate Venture Capitalists in the mid 1990s. During this period, Corporate Venturing, or venture capital in the large corporation, was just beginning to emerge as a new model of growth. Corporate executives observed venture capital firms investing in technological advances using risk capital and intellectual property in high technology fields. In many cases, they noticed members of their own firm leave the large company and create a new high potential venture, sometimes in competition with the parent. These new companies competed in the same space and pursued the same customers as the large company. In a few extreme cases the newly created public offerings had a market value that was greater than the parent from which they left just a few years earlier. Clearly, executives at large companies need to do something to help stem this departure of growth. We believe the SEU can assist.

There are a few large companies that have already experimented with an SEU template, and many more that have utilized some aspects of this model. It is really not a radical departure of existing growth templates, but rather a compilation of successful attributes borrowed from prior models from the past. However, the successful implementation of the SEU depends on a number of factors including: corporate culture, market conditions and other existing growth models. It is not a model to be used by every major public company, but could provide some benefit to many.

Executives at large public organizations need a new model of growth and should be interested in this book. Entrepreneurial employees and potential partners outside the organization can also receive benefit. Indeed, anyone who either works at a large company, does business with a large company, or would like to someday partner with a large company might potentially benefit from issues discussed in this book. Again, the limitations of implementation are largely a function of the corporate culture and the perceived need to adapt a new methodology of growth. Most organizations will likely encounter enormous resistance to change given existing incentives to continue on the same predictable path.

The new model rewards risk-taking and provides incentives to those who develop and expand upon the firm's intellectual capital. Ideally, the new growth template leverages the intellectual capital, distribution networks and cheap access made available by the parent organization yet is not encumbered by self-dealing or bureaucracy lingering in the parent culture. The SEU model is flexible enough so that growth opportunities can come from outside the large firm, or be generated from members within. Further, it enables middle managers to take advantage of small deals so that senior officers are not distracted with minutia from relatively insignificant issues.

Individuals within the organization should be attracted to the concept of the SEU since it gives them a convenient opportunity to live out an entrepreneurial dream without assuming all of the burdens of establishing an entirely new venture (i.e., raising risk capital and creating new intellectual property). Entrepreneurs running businesses external to the large, public organization will find the SEU template a simple method for establishing new business partnerships and extending their strategic direction. In both situations the risk of the new venture should be lower than the risk in developing a venture independent of the parent. Since the new venture will be associated with a parent organization that already has a business presence and infrastructure, without incorporating the high corporate overhead, the potential return should also be higher. Consequently, the SEU concept should create value for both the members of the venture as well as the parent organization.

Although it is likely that no single (small) SEU will, by itself, result in a measurable impact to the large, publicly traded parent organization, the growth of a portfolio of numerous, small and diversified SEU ventures could easily surpass the net contributions of a few enormous (non SEU) projects. As part of a diversified approach, the large organization should pursue growth both from traditional research and development and venture initiatives as well as SEU ventures. With respect to the latter, it is important that the SEU structure be established by senior management to allow independence and the opportunity to grow without undue influence from external parties.

Our research began in the mid 1990s when we first initiated interviews with Corporate Venture capitalists (we had interviews over three years) and then developed into a theoretical model in the late 1990s. We refined this concept while engaged in full time research at Harvard (at the Harvard Business School as well as the John F. Kennedy School of Government and Harvard Law Schools) and have since developed this concept. There were a number of faculty at Harvard that provided insight to this book, though they are, of course, absolved from any blame or errors included within. These include: Professor Hall and Professor Sebenius (both from Harvard Business School), Professor Mnookin (Harvard Law School), and Professor Gergen (Kennedy School of Government). Each of them provided insights that were very beneficial in developing our models. In addition to our empirical analysis at Harvard we gained additional insight in this subject from many research projects that we assigned as faculty at Babson College. In total, we received input generated from over 100 projects including more than three hundred Babson Graduate and Undergraduate students.

This project began in 1995 and ended in 2003. Corporate venturing has changed appreciably during this time period along with other models of corporate growth. The impetus for organizations to grow will continue irrespective of time period. However, methodologies will vary depending on market dynamics and opportunity availability. Applications suggested in the following pages have been primarily designed for individuals conducting business with large, publicly traded companies. It is possible, perhaps even likely, that extensions or derivations of these models might also apply to governmental bodies and private companies. Ultimately the successful approach to corporate venturing requires a careful blend of talent, financing and opportunity. The key is to ensure that value is being created in the marketplace and that the rewards are being fairly allocated to the satisfaction of all stakeholders involved. This book has been prepared with the spirit of these principles in mind.

1

GROW SMARTER OR DIE: THE FORMATION OF A STRATEGIC ENTREPRENEURIAL UNIT (SEU)

"Grow smarter or die." That's the stark choice facing corporate leaders today. And seldom has growth seemed so difficult to attain. Global competition has increased and capital providers have lost their appetite for risk. Worse, the very incentive and motivational structure of large corporations often rewards senior executives and middle managers to conspire against growth. Senior executives, knowing their time at the top may be limited, too often make decisions with a short-term payoff in mind, rather than seeking the long-term health of the enterprise. This encourages them to accelerate compensation through company stock options or "cash out" through merger and acquisition (M&A) activity. Can't large

1

companies learn to grow another way? Greed in the corporate and financial communities seems to have gotten completely out of control with reports of self-dealings becoming commonplace at previously venerable institutions such as Enron, Merrill Lynch, WorldCom, Arthur Andersen, and Imclone. Impropriety has reached senior executives, celebrities, and former leaders in a variety of communities with charges pertaining to executive compensation and shareholder goal misalignment being the common theme. Middle managers, meanwhile, realizing that no big payday awaits them, frequently adopt a strategy of bureaucratic stalemate. This helps them avoid blame, preserve their jobs, and get through the day without major headaches. But adding managerial overhead without compensating benefits (i.e., cost reductions or revenue enhancements) only exacerbates a deteriorating corporate state or weakens an otherwise successful situation. Consequently, both senior and middle management contribute to the malaise of corporate growth. Given the existing compensation and incentive structures inherent in large companies and the evolution toward more short-term orientation, perhaps it should not be surprising that few large companies were able to sustain long-term growth. After a strong growth spurt, many large, publicly traded companies tend to enter into a long stage of mediocrity. Although a handful of companies have been able to sustain their existence for 100 and even as much as 200 years, on average, after about 50 to 60 years, most large, publicly traded companies either merge out of existence or gradually go out of business altogether.

But what if there were a way for corporations to rejuvenate themselves and tap into an entrepreneurial spirit that filled the early days of their existence?

There is a way to extend the corporate life—the Strategic Entrepreneurial Unit (SEU). Properly set up and managed, the SEU not only offers many corporations a mechanism for continual renewal, it also alters the structure of corporate incentives, giving senior executives, middle managers, and line employees strong inducement to defer short-term advantage. The model focuses on enhancing the long-term health of the enterprise through strategic affiliations with many small companies. Essentially, the SEU template provides an opportunity for entrepreneurs, either internal or external to the large organization, to partner with the big company. This facility creates high-potential growth ventures leveraging the brand, intellectual property, and infrastructure of the parent without burdening the new SEU venture with the cost structure, corporate culture, or politicking of the large company. But this format is not for all companies and is not a panacea for poor management, institutional malaise, or an industrial decline.

Corporate executives may be loath to adopt a new model of growth that is still being tested. However, the SEU concept is only a modest departure from conventional means of structuring, operating, and financing entrepreneurial ventures and takes the best attributes of older, relatively successful models. Given the radical departure of financing and growing new ventures in the mid-to-late 1990s (i.e., dot.com explosion) and the problems that ensued, shouldn't executives re-examine the manner in which to fund new ventures? We believe it is time to return to fundamental growth models and build in entrepreneurial incentives leading to long-term growth. There is no better time to test it than now.

The SEU: A New Model of Growth

The SEU arrangement is distinguished by its reliance on the use of intellectual property, distribution mechanisms, or human resources within the parent organization, while it resides outside the traditional arena of research and development (R&D).

The concept of the SEU emerged from conversations with Corporate Venture Capitalists in the mid 1990s. During this period Corporate Venturing, or venture capital (VC) in the large corporation, was just beginning to emerge as a new model of growth. Corporate executives observed VC firms investing in technological advances using risk capital and intellectual property in high-technology fields. In many cases, they noticed members of their own firm leave the large company and create a new high-potential venture, sometimes in competition with the parent. These new companies competed in the same space and pursued the same customers as the large company. Clearly, executives from the large company saw this as a lost opportunity and an unnecessary reduction in market share. Arguably, the greater potential loss to the large firm could be observed through stock appreciation in the new, independent ventures. During the late 1990s many new high-technology ventures went public in an initial public offering (IPO). Given the exuberance of the dot.com market, in some cases the newly created public offerings had a market value that was greater than the parent from which they left just a few years earlier! To latch onto this new wave of growth and to stem the outflow of corporate intellectual property, executives from large companies created their own internal VC units. Their plan was to initiate entrepreneurial, high-growth ventures within the large firm and to grow corporate market share and shareholder value. These new, high-growth units were known in the marketplace as Corporate Venturing departments, and by the late 1990s they collectively managed billions of dollars in large-company risk capital. However, within five or six years, most of this risk capital had dried up, and with it, the promise for strategic growth and corporate expansion. Much of this sector's demise relates to poor market conditions. Clearly, when the overall market falls into a deep recession, it is difficult to grow in harsh economic conditions. But many of the problems can also be traced to inconsistencies in the manner in which company officials attempt to grow the large firm. In particular, compensation and incentives within large companies do not necessarily reward long-term value creation for all stakeholders, but may provide an opportunity for a small number of people to exert considerable energies for self-dealings and unique compensation. The SEU approach attempts to harness the positive energies surrounding new entrepreneurial units and share the incremental value creation in an equitable fashion. Much of its model derives from applied market research and empirical analysis. In the final analysis, the model is less about an intricate, complex algorithm and more about applying good common sense. It uses an incentive-based approach and presumes that if the proper structure and incentives are in place, the desired behaviors should follow. The development of this model and the rationale for its orientation follow.

Between 1995 and 1996, Corporate Venturing activities and procedures were just beginning to develop and gather momentum among *Fortune* 500 companies. Extensive survey data[1] confirms that many of the problems and concerns were problems associated with "Corporate Culture" and "internal politics." Other problems cited included apprehension about compensation or incentive/motivation for participants in the deals as well as managers at the firm and in the VC unit. Finally, despite the formation of a new VC unit within the firm, the corporate venturing participants reported situations in

---

1. We prepared a survey on industry practice, compensation, and equity distributions and approached Corporate Venturing officers at 31 of the *Fortune* 500 companies for their experiences in this new endeavor. As we were beginning to hear from our survey participants about impending problems, the following year we followed up with another survey and expanded our database to include an additional 16 new entrants to the field.

which employees left the large firm to start or join a new independent venture. These former employees were able to generate a better deal with the parent, after having left the company, compared to what they would have received had they continued on as employees! Thus, in some cases, individuals were given (unintentionally) economic incentive to leave the large firm and take their intellectual property with them! Corporate Venture Capitalists shared some of their frustrations that they experienced with other managers, employees, and venture capitalists outside the firm. These insights helped us craft a new path of research and a new template of corporate growth. The approach attempts to utilize the inexpensive capital available within the large firm coinciding with a (presumed) lower cost structure available in a smaller (i.e., low overhead), new independent strategic venture. More important, the structure provides compensation and incentives commensurate with the risk in the new venture, which also reflected unique contributions to the deal. The final template combines parts from many existing growth models and from our research over the past seven years. Although the SEU is partly a theoretical model, it has a place in corporate growth and long-term value creation for large companies that can produce many small-size deals. It's really a small twist to many different models from the past. However, before you consider why organizations need to pursue corporate renewal through an alternative growth extension, examine why corporations need renewing in the first place.

Why Corporate America Needs a New Growth Model

There are a variety of reasons for managers to consider a new start-up venture beyond the obvious urge to break in on the ground floor. Growth through capital investment has been a primary driver for a long time and continues today. Over the past 20 years, firms invested in ventures of all types, including strategic investments, that leveraged existing corporate technologies as well as investments solely for financial pursuit. In the latter case, the proximity to the core business did not seem to matter so long as the desired financial return was achieved. During the mid-to-late 1990s, it appeared that corporate venturing investments seemed to shift away from "strategic deals" to "financial deals." In fact, one corporate venturing officer explained the move away from strategic to financial goals with the statement "there is nothing strategic about losing money." This particular statement epitomizes the move toward financial return at precisely the time when organizations were flush with cash and there was an abundance of attractive investment options. However, the disappearance of attractive investments in the once robust dot.com and telecommunications industries coupled with a severe worldwide recession from 2000 to 2003 changed the landscape of corporate venturing deal flow and capital availability. Activity during this time period hit bottom. But the type and number of transactions often reflects market conditions and opportunities. The economic and strategic motivation of corporate officers to create wealth through new initiatives continues, irrespective of market conditions, and should blossom when conditions are ripe.

Although much of the motivation to create new venture relates to wealth creation, there are at least five primary reasons to formulate and start a venture in addition to pure financial gain. These reasons (which are discussed at greater length later) are often inter-related but include the following five:

1. Strategic expansion of the firm into new areas

2. Technological acquisition

3. New product development

4. New market entry

5. Cultural change implementation

The preceding list summarizes a few reasons why new ventures help develop the organization for purposes other than earning a financial return. Ultimately, however, the new initiatives need to earn a financial return or they will result in a financial drain on the entire organization to the detriment of all stakeholders. Further, the problem often is not so much how to initiate new ventures, but rather how to implement them *within* the organization in a way that allows the new ventures to have an opportunity to grow and flourish. Existing structures within large organizations often make it difficult to create the excitement of a new venture. Further, if internal management is averse to change, there will be hurdles to overcome. For example, delays regarding resource allocation, rewards, and control may all strangle the new venture or prevent it from ever being created in the first place.

What the SEU Needs to Succeed

Large, public organizations need a new model of growth. The new model should reward risk-taking and provide incentives to those who develop and expand on the firm's intellectual capital. Ideally, the new growth template should leverage the intellectual capital, distribution networks, and cheap access made available by the parent organization but not be encumbered by self-dealing or bureaucracy lingering in the parent culture. The SEU model is flexible enough so that growth opportunities can come from outside the large firm or be generated from members within.

Further, it enables middle managers to take advantage of small deals so that senior officers are not distracted with minutia from relatively insignificant issues.

The SEU model works best with small deals, ranging in size value from $100,000 to $2,000,000. Larger deals require (or command) the attention of senior management and will not easily be left alone for middle managers or outsiders to control. The primary purpose of the SEU should be to leverage the strategic value created by the parent organization and to create a high-potential venture with the aid of entrepreneurs within, and perhaps even more likely, outside the organization. SEUs should be affiliated with the parent and utilize the parent's resources (i.e., capital, intellectual property, infrastructure) whenever it can be applied in an efficient manner, but should be managed as an independent organization, akin to an external business. Individuals within the organization should be attracted to the concept of the SEU since it gives them a convenient opportunity to live out an entrepreneurial dream without assuming all of the burdens of establishing an entirely new venture (i.e., raising risk capital and creating new intellectual property). Entrepreneurs running businesses external to the large, public organization will find the SEU template a simple method for establishing new business partnerships and extending their strategic direction. In both situations, the risk of the new venture should be lower than the risk in developing a venture independent of the parent. Since the new venture will be associated with a parent organization that already has a business presence and infrastructure, without incorporating the high corporate overhead, the potential return should also be higher. Consequently, the SEU concept should create value for both the members of the venture as well as the parent organization.

Although it is likely that no single (small) SEU will, by itself, result in a measurable impact to the large, publicly traded parent organization, the growth of a portfolio of numerous, small, and diversified SEU ventures could easily surpass the net contributions of a few enormous (non-SEU) projects. As part of a diversified approach, the large organization should pursue growth from both traditional R&D and venture initiatives, as well as SEU ventures. With respect to the latter, it is important that the SEU structure be established by senior management to allow independence and to provide the opportunity to grow without undue influence from external parties. The SEU model requires insulation from self-serving venture capitalists, dealmakers, research analysts, and other consultants or advisors who might drive the SEU's management into behavior that serves special short-term interests at the expense of long-term wealth creation.

What the SEU Can Achieve

This SEU model attempts to overcome problems associated with compensation disincentives and misdirected growth that may serve only the needs of a few stakeholders. Furthermore, it attempts to remove any biases resulting from venture capitalists, investment bankers, and management focusing on short-term deal harvests at the expense of long-term strategic growth. The model creates an incentive-based environment that hinges on all parties working in their own best interests. All parties to the deal focus on the incremental value being created in the deal, net of the necessary costs associated with risk capital, intellectual property, and human talent. Pure wealth creation occurs only after all of the parties have been adequately compensated for their contributions.

As in any new venture, the associated rewards should be commensurate with the risks. The risks could exceed any that participants in the venture have shouldered while under the parent's wing, but those who help create new wealth with new resources should be entitled to exceptional rewards. For example, individuals (including employees, financiers, and advisors) who forego some salary, benefits, or job security in the short term should be entitled to higher compensation in the future if the venture becomes successful. Further, if the parent organization lends financial resources, intellectual property, or other strategic infrastructure benefits (e.g., distribution) to the SEU venture, then its stakeholders (e.g., shareholders) ought to receive a reasonable financial reward as well. Unlike most new large-company growth ventures where company employees do not have a financial stake or economic risk in the success (or failure) of the new initiative, investors in SEU ventures are placing a financial wager on people who are sacrificing real cash dollars and who are effectively betting on themselves to make the ventures succeed. If management has done its job, it has already hired the best and brightest available in the marketplace. The SEU template now requires management to create a facility that nurtures some of this talent in a creative, productive manner.

Anatomy of an SEU

The basic structure of an SEU owes much to the unit's agreement with and strategic orientation to the parent or large organization. Without a strategic fit, the new venture might still be feasible but falls under the umbrella of financial investment.

Figure 1.1 shows the formation of an SEU—entrepreneurs within the organization.

To ensure that information flows appropriately between the parent and the new venture, a third party in a new role serves as the gatekeeper of confidential information. This third party, or

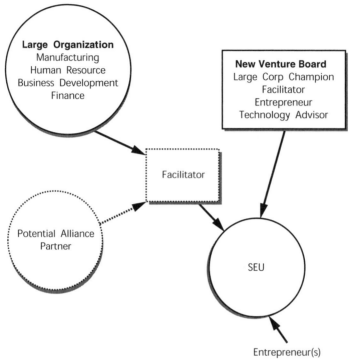

Figure 1.1   Parties to an SEU venture

Facilitator, will be responsible for negotiating the terms of the deal and handling sensitive issues like protection of intellectual property and conflict resolution. The sole responsibility of the third party should be to represent the fair interests of all stakeholders and to maximize the value of the deal—not necessarily the interests of either the parent or the entrepreneur(s).

The Facilitator has a number of tasks including confidential deal screening and review. As an administrative linchpin, the Facilitator helps coordinate other services that the new venture may require that can be efficiently handled by the parent or other service provider. This includes bringing in new entrepreneurial or task-oriented talent as well as administrative responsibilities. Since any new venture frequently has many changing dynamics including funding, development of intellectual property, strategic alliances, personnel mobility, liquidity, and strategic alliances, the third-party Facilitator also fills the role of overseer of conflict resolution.

The presence of the Facilitator is central to the SEU model and makes it very different from traditional venturing models.

The Traditional VC Model

The most common venturing model places the venture capitalist or corporate venturing party in the middle. By contrast, the SEU approach eliminates the potential biases of the VC or corporate agent and creates a new post that has loyalty to protect the best interests of all participants in the deal. The Facilitator receives both fee income and a small equity stake, but cannot force liquidity through an IPO or strategic sale. This is an important difference that removes a potentially destructive conflict of interest.

Although the SEU model does not completely replace traditional models, it does offer management an interesting alternative to consider. It eliminates the greed sometimes associated with the present VC model and reduces the myopic mindset sometimes found among participants wanting to harvest a venture prematurely.

The harvest-at-all-costs approach to VC investment directs resources into a complex shell game designed to mix and match human talent and corporate distribution networks and finances for the sole purpose of converting existing assets into a short-term profit position. Whether or not true economies of scale or intellectual property have been realized may have been completely irrelevant to financiers of the past decade. For example, the M&A focus of the 1990s not only failed to achieve the desired economies of scale, but in most cases the abrupt combination of firms in the name of growth disrupted well-organized cultures and created diseconomies of scale. These diseconomies resulted from the combined parties not getting along, and from the increased borrowing costs and investment banker and financier fees associated with the consolidations. Many consolidations and acquisitions were financial disasters. It took a while for the market to figure this out, however. By the time the market realized precisely what had happened, it was too late to reverse the situation back to its old status. The combined company had already disassembled the separate organizational structures and dismantled the independent operating units.

Short Term Is Out—Long Term is In

The SEU model creates an opportunity for an external party to filter the deals and in an unbiased manner help negotiate the terms of the deal. It removes the administrative burden for management to watch over and manage each deal and allows entrepreneurs (from within and outside) to develop strategic links with the large, public company. Moreover, as we discuss in greater depth later, because this concept is first being applied to large, publicly traded companies, it eliminates the enormous costs and biases associated with an organizational harvest. Entrepreneurs and other stakeholders who require liquidity (cash) will be allowed an opportunity to tap their created wealth, without resorting to an outright sale or liquidation of the organization. Thus, key participants to the deal can focus their day-to-day efforts on long-term value creation rather than driving toward an immediate harvest opportunity. This is another important distinction from the classic venturing model and we believe a key advantage to the SEU.

A Fresh Perspective

Many large, public companies can indeed grow more efficiently and effectively, but growth will require an entirely new perspective. Implementation may also require some career risk to participants, but not without its compensating factors. Ultimately, individuals engaged within an entrepreneurial orientation should find employment more satisfying and lucrative if they know that they can potentially earn an equity stake in their business unit. In many respects they will be working for themselves in their own business, but will have the added protection and security of being partnered with a major organization. As long as wealth is created, the new arrangement should be deemed successful. This is our strategic pursuit.

Over the past few decades, new models of growth and management approaches have gone in and out of style. In this approach, not all members of the firm need to be entrepreneurs, but the overall firm needs to provide entrepreneurial rewards for those willing to seek them. Ultimately, the company can achieve its targets more efficiently by allowing smaller units within to operate independently and in an entrepreneurial manner. These small entrepreneurial groups (both inside and outside the firm) will keep costs lower and operate more efficiently once they have the economic incentives to perform in this manner.

Large Companies *Should* Win

Large companies can win, and given their human and financial resource advantages, *should* win. But they can't do it the old-fashioned way. For too long large companies have been slogging along with stakeholders, both internal and external to the organization, each trying to "game" the system to their own personal advantage. This needs to stop. These problems occur in a large organization because few are really accountable for anything other than a narrow cog within the large wheel. This doesn't happen in a small, entrepreneurial organization. In a small organization, the owners know precisely which members are adding value to the entity and which members are not. They know how to motivate key people and know precisely how their products and services compare with competitors. They have the entire picture of the business model, for all its beauty marks and warts, and generally have an idea where they would like to take the business, even if they don't have the wherewithal to get there. Large businesses don't operate in this manner. Perhaps they would operate better if they did. Large companies need an environment that successfully integrates and recognizes each member's relative contributions. Equally important, they need a system that efficiently and equitably handles compensation and motivation on an individual basis. In short, big businesses need to alter their model of growth or risk the decline that has affected all other large businesses in the past. In the absence of major institutional change, big businesses should not expect to extend their traditional life cycle. They will grow, become mature, and die.

Large, public companies can turn the tide if they harness their considerable resources properly and breathe life into their growth units. But changes that we propose will not come without difficult choices. Moreover, the SEU model is absolutely not for everybody. Senior managers will have to relax, even concede, control of many strategic operating units. This is especially true for the small groups that they may not currently even know or care about. They will need to have confidence in the same capital market principles that help create their organization's success initially. They will need to help develop a facility that allows its members to think, act, and behave in an entrepreneurial manner. Much of the risks and rewards should accrue to its members, though the parent will receive its rewards for overall integration. The large, public company can succeed and extend its natural life cycle. But it needs to create a new growth facility that will enable this possibility to occur.

Our recommendation for this dilemma is the implementation of SEUs. This approach will require a different corporate mindset and a different corporate orientation. Furthermore, to grow most efficiently and effectively, the large company may need to transform some of its operations into a series of small, entrepreneurial units. In short, we believe that for the large company to get bigger it needs to *grow* smaller.

2

THE CORPORATE LIFE CYCLE: WHY CAN'T BUSINESSES GROW FOREVER?

"Businesses get big, grow old, and die,
and there is nothing as a CEO that I can do to change it."

Fortune 500 CEO speaking to
Harvard Business School Class, April 2000

Is Corporate Death Inevitable?

Big businesses grow, mature, and decline, but is there anything that management can do to help change this trend? Generally speaking, it is difficult to keep companies vibrant. Despite significant economic advantages that large, public companies appear to have over other organizational entities, the eventual decline in operations appears inevitable. Moreover, so long as incentive systems remain in place as they currently exist, there is no compelling reason why this pattern will change.

But shouldn't large companies get bigger and stronger over time? With increased size, don't large organizations gain economies of scale in production, marketing savvy, and distribution? *Shouldn't* large companies become even more dominant over time with increased brand recognition, management expertise, and access to cheap capital? These arguments suggest that large companies *should* get stronger and more efficient over time. However, the evidence shows otherwise.

Large, public companies often experience strong *revenue* growth from year to year, but it is the young companies, not old, that experience *common stock* growth (i.e., appreciation). Growth in all organizational areas is not necessarily beneficial to the long-term stability of the firm. In fact, depending on the type of growth and the *manner* in which it was accomplished, growth in some areas (e.g., revenue growth) may come at the expense of other stakeholder interest groups (e.g., stockholders, or debt holders).

In the end, there may be little that management can accomplish that will prevent corporate failure due to poor economic conditions, product obsolescence, or individual impropriety. However, it may be possible to extend corporate life by channeling more of the organizational stakeholders' energy and focus back into the company. Corporations can consider an alternative compensation and incentive mechanism that shares some of the wealth (or equity) with the entrepreneurs who are responsible for the wealth creation and leave the balance to those who supply some of the venture financing and intellectual property. This is not necessarily a completely original concept, nor is it an idea that has not been attempted in some way in the past. For many years management has attempted to implant entrepreneurial behavior and excitement within its corporate walls. In essence, this approach applies a new twist to an old dilemma.

Corporate Renewal Programs

Corporate renewal programs are not recent innovations. These approaches have arguably been around for at least 30 or more years. During the 1960s, companies such as Gulf and Western pursued corporate growth through acquisition. They diversified their corporate holdings by acquiring companies in different industries with relatively high growth prospects and high price-to-earnings (P/E) ratios. Part of the hope was that the high P/E ratio from the new acquired company would carry over to the entire organization. If this occurred then the entire company would rise quickly in value, thus providing confirmation for the acquisition. During the 1970s a new term, *intrapreneurship,* was coined for entrepreneurial growth within the company. High-growth companies such as Digital Equipment would attempt to create wealth through new initiatives within the organization. The parent owned 100% of the equity and funded new ventures with existing "entrepreneurs." Sometimes the ventures moved to a separate building to foster creativity and keep it apart from the influence of the parent. Although new companies were not spun out in an IPO, as they did years later at ThemoElectron, there was great excitement with the distinct new product orientation.

During the 1980s companies focused on creating value through financial techniques. These included (but were not limited to): hostile takeovers with junk bonds, leveraged buyouts, securitization of company assets, and other financial asset repackagings that came under the heading of "Financial Engineering." Corporate values would rise and fall very quickly depending on the supply and demand of capital and the urgency of parties to complete a transaction. However, little could prepare us for the extraordinary events of the mid-to-late 1990s. During this period companies introduced Corporate Venturing groups that invested risk capital into new corporate initiative. The intent was to create new risk ventures that could be sold off in a strategic sale or presented as an IPO candidate. During the 1990s entrepreneurial individuals left big companies and created their own new ventures in competition with the parent. Not only did the parent organization have to contend with a new competitor, but in the process it lost great value for its shareholders in a new, focused upstart.

Now there is a new category referred to as "Corporate Entrepreneurship." Since this term has become popularized in the post-dot.com era, there has been relatively little risk capital or activity to monitor. However, there is an opportunity to apply some of the lessons learned from the past to a new set of companies. The approach takes the excitement and some of the organizational culture of the 1970s Intrapreneurship model, applies a corporate venturing initiative approach set up in the 1990s, and applies a "financial engineering" orientation of the 1980s in allocating rewards to the different stakeholders. This approach, discussed in greater detail later, basically gives an equity (or ownership) interest and operational control to the individuals who are capable of creating high-potential growth ventures. By creating this structure within the big company, individuals will be motivated to remain with their parent companies, rather than leave to create their own venture or join another group. Moreover, with the proper structure, entrepreneurs who are not currently affiliated with the large company will be attracted to bring their energy and creativity to the big company for mutual opportunity. However, this is a goal and not yet a common practice. Large, publicly held companies, for reasons covered later, have traditionally been unsuccessful in appreciably extending corporate life through new, strategic directions.

Corporate Life Cycle

Some large companies, such as Lucent Technologies or Enron, experience an extremely short duration among the elite companies in the *Fortune* 500. However, their corporate fate is atypical of the norm. Most of the large, public companies that fall from grace tend to do so over a relatively long, painful process. By the time these mature companies file for Chapter 11 bankruptcy protection they have undergone massive corporate restructurings, corporate layoffs, and significant asset sales or divestitures. Since they are big companies, with potentially many jobs at stake, there is considerable popular press coverage and few details that are not deemed worthy for public scrutiny. During the year 2002 alone, 186 public companies filed for bankruptcy protection with debt amounting to $368 billion. The prior year witnessed a then-record $259 billion debt level in bankrupties. Some of the large companies that filed for bankruptcy experienced corporate impropriety or scandal (Enron, WorldCom, Adelphia Communications, Arthur Andersen), but not most. Some of the companies were organizational super stars during an earlier period in the 1960s, 1970s, or 1980s and were now suffering 20 to 40 years later. For example, Kmart, United Airlines, and Conseco all filed for bankruptcy in 2002. There are many other companies with a celebrated past, such as Xerox and Motorola, who have come very close to financial jeopardy and have required major corporate restructurings to fight for survival.

Corporations are established as an economic entity that can theoretically last forever. In fact, the permanence of the organizational entity is an important demarcation between companies that are incorporated and sole proprietorships and partnerships. The latter organizational structures expire when one of the parties leaves the organization or expires. This is not so with a company that is incorporated; it continues on irrespective of the health or participation of its shareholders. Further, unlike a sole proprietorship or partnership, individuals within a corporation cannot be directly sued. They have limited liability. However, despite the theoretical underpinnings of the corporate shell, many academics and practitioners believe that organizations have a finite product and industrial life cycle. Interestingly enough, even though corporations can last forever and live well beyond the life of an individual (as they do in some cases), on average large, publicly traded companies seem to expire just like human life (see Figure 2.1). Some industrial life cycles may last decades, whereas others (such as the dot.coms) may move from start-up to bust within a fraction of that period. The life cycle theory suggests that corporate and industrial decline is predictable and part of a natural existence. However, organizations can extend the traditional life cycle through product innovation and strategic partnering.

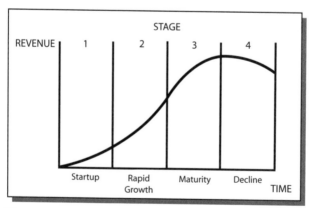

Figure 2.1 Organizational life cycle

The Evidence

Out of almost 18,000 companies trading on the New York Stock Exchange, American Stock Exchange companies, NASDAQ, and OTC, General Electric emerged as the *one* company (that was not run by the founder) that seemed to offer the best track record of consistently outperforming all other groups over the period 1980–2000. During this time period, many other firms had also performed well. But no other company consistently outperformed all other public companies for the 20-year period. Long-term founders/Chief Executive Officers (CEOs) were more likely to outperform the industry benchmarks than most other companies. For example, Microsoft (Bill Gates), Oracle (Larry Ellison), Dell Computer (Michael Dell), and Intel (Andy Grove), were among other founders/CEOs whose companies experienced unusually strong, comparative performance over a long time period. Founder-led companies often experience a different culture, goal orientation, and style compared to other large, public companies. This stems from the excitement/drive, compensation incentives, and watchful eye of the entrepreneurial founder, and perhaps it is these useful traits that an organization loses after the founder departs.

There is a lesson here for big companies. If more people created their own little business initiatives within an organization, perhaps employees would turn into entrepreneurial partners and growth for the combined entity would grow at an unprecedented rate. However, before embarking on a mission to help extend corporate life, it is first important to identify and consider how large companies evolve/grow and how long they can be expected to last.

How Big and Old Do Public Companies Get?

How old do public companies get? This is a question that addresses the life cycle issue and puts some perspective on whether or not, from a practical standpoint, large, public companies get bigger and stronger over time. Due to the abundance of M&As over the years, the actual age of each firm of the *Fortune* 500, or the largest 500 firms in the United States, was subject to some level of misinterpretation. The *Fortune* 500 companies have an average age of around 54 years. Given the age of the United States, and the fact that some companies could have been started in Europe and Asia and then brought over to the United States, some may find this surprising and expect these large companies to be older. The oldest, large, publicly traded company in the United States is the Bank of New York at 220 years of age. Only two other companies, Fleet Bank (formerly Bank of Boston) at 213 years and Cigna at 201 years, meet or exceed 200 years of age. Even if other large, public companies can demonstrate a linkage to earlier periods, there may be little incentive to do so. As companies grow larger and prosper, they may become more likely targets for lawsuits and attacks by special interest groups. For example, Fleet Bank and Aetna Insurance were named to lawsuits resulting from former slave trading and insurance activities conducted 200 years ago by acquired organizations. Given their size, customer base, and exposure to high-profile embarrassment, indirect slave reparations and imposed fines may be forthcoming.

Interestingly, the problems associated with Aetna and Fleet Bank may represent one reason why large, high-profile companies do not survive in the long term. Given the potential for unlimited damages and the one-sided nature of litigation (i.e., large companies can lose large amounts but generally cannot win much from individuals or small organizations), large, deep-pocketed companies are likely to lose some significant lawsuits over a long period of time (i.e., 100 or more years). High-profile lawsuits and/or corporate impropriety have either destroyed successful companies or pushed them to the brink of disaster. These include RJR (tobacco liability), Exxon (Valdez oil spill), Union Carbide (Bhopal explosion), Texaco (Getty Oil), Manville (asbestos), AH Robbins (toxic shock), Enron (impropriety), WorldCom (accounting impropriety), Adelphia (impropriety), and Arthur Andersen (impropriety). Periodically, one new form of litigation can bring down an entire industry. For example, during an 18-month time span between 2000 and 2001, six *Fortune* 500 companies filed for bankruptcy as a result of asbestos litigation (Owens Corning, Babcock & Wilcox, Armstrong World Industries, WR Grace, GAF, and USG). A few years earlier, Federal Mogul and Manville filed for bankruptcy due to the same problem. This may be just one additional reason why many high-profile, large companies do not survive forever, but in recent years it seems to be a significant factor. As mentioned earlier, organizations that incorporate protect individuals from being sued (i.e., limited liability). However, the corporate entity can still be sued and the evidence suggests that such lawsuits frequently harm otherwise successful operations. We illustrate the actual profile of large companies next.

Typical Profile of a *Fortune* 500 Company?

More than 80% of *Fortune* 500 companies are younger than 100 years with only 92 (out of 500) having a longer existence (see Figure 2.2). Approximately one half of all *Fortune* 500 companies are less than 50 years of age and more than one third are less than

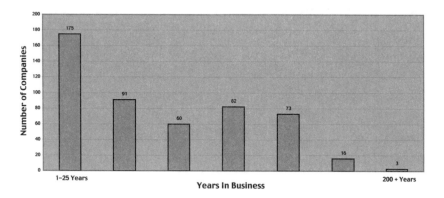

Figure 2.2   *Fortune* 500 companies over 200 years

25 years of age. Because this profile of the *Fortune* 500 implied a young firm bias, we went back to our common stock and balance sheet data to search for a consistent pattern. The stock returns during recent years were appreciably higher among the younger firms. Further, the revenue and profit growth through internal expansion, otherwise known as "organic growth," was appreciably higher for younger firms compared to older firms. The fact is, most publicly traded companies in America do not continue to grow bigger and stronger over time. Rather, it appears that large companies tend to grow older and weaker. More important, the 500 largest firms do not provide insight into how large, older companies *should* behave.

On balance, there exists a trend toward large, public companies decaying over time. There were a few exceptions to the rule (e.g., even at over 150 years old, Dow Corning, for a short time period, experienced success with fiber optics) but the trend generally was that larger companies did not gain financial strength over time. This evidence points to an industry life cycle, but does not specifically point to patterns of major transformations among many companies.

Why Don't Big Companies Grow Forever? Let's Ask the Experts

Many experts think that big, public companies eventually decline because they don't adapt very well to innovation or technological advances. Change, flexibility, and adaptation, they argue, provide the recipe to survival. This would suggest that old public companies have made the move into other industries or lines of business. Alternatively, perhaps, large, successful companies would be observed in a constant state of motion.

Large, public companies do not provide much support to demonstrate that significant change occurs through internal expansion or organic growth models. There is plenty of evidence, however, that large, publicly traded companies are attempting to change through M&A activity. Growth through acquisition does not often create value for the buying companies' shareholders. However, growth through organic (internal expansion) means often creates long-term value for the shareholders. It is these types of situations that may create worthy growth templates for other corporations to follow. In a search for companies that extended their corporate life cycle through innovative growth measures, Microsoft offers a useful example of how it might apply. Other examples illustrate applications for companies in differing stages of their life cycle.

Extending the Life Cycle: A Few Cases in Point

The life cycle shown here is the same life cycle shown earlier. However, it is categorized here in five data points from A to E for illustrative purposes that show a theoretical extension to the classic life cycle curve from A to G and C to F (see Figure 2.3). Clearly,

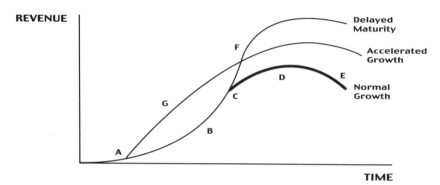

Figure 2.3 High growth extensions

corporate managers would hope to extend their company life cycle along the curve shown near point "A" or near point "C." But as you will see, such a theoretical extension is not so simple in practice.

Company at Point "A"

At first glance, the company at point "A" does not appear to have any reason to be thinking about extending its life cycle to point "G." Most individuals experiencing the growth of company "A" have their hands full with all of the issues confronting steep growth as it currently exists. Generally speaking, an individual who is at point "A" in the life cycle is not worrying about points "B," "C," "D," or "E." The slope of the curve at point "A" suggests that the company is already experiencing strong growth in revenue in a relatively short time period. Why would any individual in company "A's" position even contemplate extending the growth cycle through a new corporate venture?

This means that the company is growing at an even faster rate (for a given amount of time) compared to the company on the slope of point "A" to point "B." Hopefully this greater growth implies more value for the key stakeholders. Several private companies have already created an extension as shown in the graph (from point "A" to point "G"). One company was itself a spinoff from a large bank in the Midwest. It began as a three-person operation and quickly grew to several hundred people. In 2001 we interviewed the company officers about their thoughts on the SEU template. One year later a couple of specialized consultants at the firm were contemplating a departure. Rather than let them leave the firm, the company created an SEU with its former employees and agreed to a revenue, profit sharing, and equity arrangement. Thus far it seems to be working for all parties and the specialized consultants are working harder than ever on "their" new firm. The new companies have collectively more growth (shown by the curve that is above the A, B, C, D, E curve) than if they had remained as one unit during the same time period.

Company at Point "B"

Arguably, if AOL, Intel, or Oracle, initiated an SEU in their first 5 to 10 years of existence, they all would be classified as Point "Bs." These companies each had explosive, organic, or internal growth throughout their early years and were on this vertical slope for a relatively long time period. Point "B" companies can leverage their growth and extend their life cycle by initiating SEUs in this stage. Palm Computing offers an interesting example.

In 1997, 3Com purchased U.S. Robotics when Jeff Hawkins was developing the Palm operating system. In early 2000, 3Com spun out Palm Computing (when it was an $11 billion company) and Jeff Hawkins and former Palm CEO Donna Dubrinsky left

Palm in 1998 and founded Handspring. This new company developed a product called Visor that operates on the Palm system. By 2002 Palm had $1.5 billion in revenue and Handspring had $270 million. Although Handspring is independent of Palm, this example shows how one high-potential venture can spin off into another venture with the same growth prospects. Further, to the extent that there are interrelations between two companies it should be possible to leverage the combined entities for mutual benefit. Over the past two decades there have been many other point "B" situations in which high-growth ventures left the parent and created competition in the same industry. The SEU template attempts to leverage this growth for the benefit of all parties.

Company at Point "C"

Few companies of the past 50 years can boast the type of wealth creation and growth of Microsoft. However, in recent years Microsoft engaged in an "SEU-type" of operation with XBox founders Kevin Bachus and Seamus Blackley to gain entry into the rapidly growing video gaming market. Microsoft provided equity incentives and risk sharing in a new arena offering revenue growth estimated to reach $30 billion. Outside talent teamed with internal staff in a separately funded venture. The economics were structured with incentives and founder/CEO Bill Gates helped negotiate the terms of the deal (akin to an *internal* facilitator). The XBox scenario that contributed over $1.3 billion in revenues to Microsoft in 2002 demonstrates how even a large, growing entity can extend its life cycle in new, innovative paths. This is represented in Figure 2.3 by moving from Point "C" to Point "F."

Company at Point "D"

Fortune 500 Pharmaceutical giant Baxter International is at a mature stage in its product and industry life cycle, but is now exploring new initiatives and mechanisms to create ventures with unique compensation and incentives. MSXI is another company that is exploring an SEU formation. When the company announced that it would be restructuring its operations and laying off some of its members, the CEO provided a few entrepreneurial employees an option of either a severance package or an equity stake in a new strategic venture. The entrepreneurs would have revenues from the parent corporation as well as another publicly traded corporation in the same industry. The parent corporation and the other large company would own a majority stake in the new venture to compensate for their intellectual property and equity investment, but the entrepreneurs would have operational control in their new company (along with their equity interest). This example shows how even a mature company may try to prolong its life cycle and accelerate growth through an SEU operation.

Company at Point "E"

Companies such as Motorola or Xerox are what many would consider point "E" type companies. They are mature organizations that are seeking some new growth initiative. After a $1 billion loss with its Iridium (global satellite) initiative, Motorola began exploring "SEU" initiatives on a much smaller scale. Motorola has considered new venture initiatives that approach an SEU, but do not yet provide all of the features of this application (e.g., no Facilitator or equity for participants). Xerox, on the other hand, has had extensive experience with SEU-type ventures (Xerox Technology Ventures) and can cite a number of successes (e.g., Documentum, ChannelBind, Document Sciences Corporation) that have assisted with its turnaround. In the past, Xerox has shared some of the equity incentives with its employees, but has not systematically institutionalized or standardized the process or introduced an external Facilitator (as described in the SEU template).

Creating a Template for Future Corporate Empires

What is the template for creating a longlasting, self-sustaining organization or empire? History demonstrates that great empires can last for hundreds, even thousands of years, yet our evidence suggests that large companies in the United States don't normally last beyond 100 years. That is not to suggest that large, international public companies should last 1,000 years, but such firms are, in many respects, growing empires. They hire hundreds of thousands of individuals and move commerce worth billions of dollars around the globe. They have an enormous impact to many individual families and societies throughout the world.

With the proper growth model, large, multinational companies can extend their corporate existence and push the average age well beyond 54 years. These firms need the appropriate incentive structure that attracts great talent and keeps it motivated for long periods of time. They cannot afford to lose key people to new ventures or competitors.

Existing growth models may currently provide economic incentive for talented agents of the firm to work toward a major company-altering situation such as an IPO, sale of assets, or M&A, but this may not create wealth in the long term. An alternative growth model may not provide all of the answers and can't possibly help all companies, but the current approach needs to be modified. Corporate America needs a template in which potential partners both within and outside the organization have economic incentive to drive toward a common purpose and goal. It needs a better model of growth. And, it needs it now. Large companies can get bigger and extend their corporate life by growing through smaller ventures. The next few chapters will provide the rationale and a step-by-step approach to setting up an SEU.

3

What's Wrong with the Current System? Compensation without Long-Term Value Creation

High Compensation without Revenues— Now That's a Problem

Reflecting on the spate of dot.com explosions and implosions during the past few years, selecting stocks based on fundamental analysis seems more difficult than ever.[1] In the late 1990s, some stocks went

---

1. Fundamental investment is an approach made famous by authors/investors Benjamin Graham and David Dodd in books such as *Security Analysis* (1934) and by Graham in *The Intelligent Investor* (1940). This approach to buying stocks requires an analysis of balance sheet and income statement data and looks for value creation based on improvements in asset growth and organization management.

up without profits and, in extreme cases, without revenues. Spirited M&A activity and soaring compensation didn't always coincide with stock price increases and the only ones who seem to have prospered were the deal makers, consultants, bankers, and executives who cashed out along the way. The current system seems broke and it's already attracting the attention of regulators. Change is inevitable and companies will need to grow revenues and compensate people in a different manner. Management can wait for new regulations or risk using old methods. Alternatively, management can pursue an SEU path now.

Part of the problem with the current system may lie in compensation that rewards stakeholders for behavior that does not create long-term value for shareholders.[2] But these highly compensated individuals may be simply taking advantage of a configuration and playing by rules that they didn't create. Each may be trying to move the company in a way that provides personal benefit at the expense of another party. And this is just a start. There may be plenty of other parties with specific biases that may not necessarily move the company forward in a path beneficial to all.

Identifying the problems is only part of the battle. Getting people to fix a situation when it runs counter to their financial best interests is appreciably more complex. However, in recent years, developments in the financial community suggest that major change may be imminent. The SEC has fined major Wall

---

2. We distinguish shareholders from "other stakeholders" because stakeholders represent the broader group that may include (among others) stockholders, employees, suppliers, debt holders, members of the community, board members, and so forth. Sometimes, the interests of all of the stakeholders may not be aligned. This means that money going to one party may come at the expense of another member in the group. This is the general problem being addressed in this opening paragraph.

Street firms over $1.4 billion in inappropriate business practices and has permanently banned certain research analysts.[3] Furthermore, senior U.S. senators and other government officials are now pushing for reform because they see self-regulation by the capital markets "as a complete abject failure."[4] Such contemplation may have been inconceivable even a few years ago. However, the poor economy early in the new millennium and the revelations of gross improprieties and conflicts of interest may provide a window of opportunity for changing compensation models.[5] The rules for growing a company are absolutely changing and senior management needs to stay current with new conditions. The first change will undoubtedly focus on money and be forced on major institutions by regulatory agencies. That is, unless companies choose to change on a voluntary basis. Compensation has been and continues to be a major issue that needs to be addressed one way or another.

---

3. In a May 1, 2003 report, Forbes.com cited fines for financial firms of $2.95 billion for 2002 and over $3 billion for 2003. On December 20, 2002, the U.S. Securities and Exchange Commission (SEC) fined some of Wall Street's largest firms $1.335 billion, including Bear Stearns, Credit Suisse Group, Deutsche Bank, Goldman Sachs, J.P. Morgan Chase, Lehman Brothers, Merrill Lynch, Morgan Stanley, Citigroup, and UBS. Salomon Smith Barney, a unit of Citigroup, will pay the largest fine of $400 million. Credit Suisse First Boston will pay $200 million with other firms paying between $80 million and $125 million. The settlement also banned two analysts from the securities business for life. This includes former Merrill Lynch & Co. Internet analyst Henry Blodget as well as Jack Grubman, who was previously the top telecommunications analyst at Salomon Smith Barney (unit of Citigroup, Inc.).

4. Quote attributed to New York Attorney General Eliot Spitzer in Reuters, May 7, 2003, "Senators Skeptical on Wall St. Settlement."

5. In one particularly egregious case, Jack Grubman allegedly used his Wall Street connections to gain his children admission to a prestigious Manhattan nursery school by changing his rating on AT&T stock to win favor from the company CEO, Sanford Weill (November 14, 2002, Forbes.com, "Weill-Grubman Dealings were Child's Play").

Money Is Not Everything—But It's Pretty Darn Important

Perhaps nothing exemplifies the over-exuberance of the 1980s and 1990s as much as the over-the-top compensation earned by executives and dealmakers. Some of these guys made big money— huge amounts of money. During the go-go years in the 1980s and 1990s, new compensation records were broken each year. First it was $100 million, then $500 million, and later $1 billion.[6] No amount of cash, bonus, or stock options seemed inappropriate. After all, compensation experts reasoned, most of the executive compensation came in the form of stock options. Since stock options could only earn money when the stock price went up, so long as the stock price increased, all parties gained. This implies that no stakeholders lose. This was the logic built into compensation plans throughout the 1980s and 1990s.

Those who disagreed with this logic would risk being shunned from the marketplace. After all, an appreciating stock market is said to establish right from wrong. The markets supposedly incorporate future expectations into the existing price and know best. In the 1990s the market had boundless energy coinciding with sky-rocketing compensation levels. It was not by coincidence. More deals create more growth, which justifies higher salaries, bonuses, and options. This was a wild ride fueled, in part, by insatiable greed and cheap financing. It was a great time to be an executive of a large company. Actually, it was a great time to be an investment

---

6. In Business Week Online (April 19, 1999), a chronology of compensation milestones are cited including: Disney CEO Michael Eisner's 1998 compensation at $577 million and Roberto Goizueta, CEO of Coca Cola, earning over $1.3 billion on his stock options.

banker, compensation consultant, venture capitalist, or average investor on the street. An unprecedented amount of money could be earned in a relatively short time period.

Whatever Goes Up...

Bad compensation mechanisms cannot be blamed for all of our stock market and economic woes. But bad compensation mechanisms were certainly a big part of this mess. Compensation mechanisms were tied in with the greed that gripped our markets. Individuals had economic incentive to behave in a manner that might not contribute to the long-run wealth creation of the organization. Another factor was that when our capital market systems gather momentum, there is little that can slow them down. Rising stock markets create new wealth, which enables companies to use inflated stock as currency to buy other companies. New infusions of risk capital then enter the market, providing funding for additional investments. With rising equity levels, companies can borrow additional bank debt, driving leverage and risk to new heights. This may result in yet another round or cycle of appreciating stock, harvests, and new investments. Reality may not set in until much later when it becomes too late to reverse a large transaction.

Once the first ripple of quarterly reports indicates that the high-profile companies missed their financial projections, things begin to unwind. This is bad news with markets adjusting quickly. Over recent years, the investment cycle of (1) invest, (2) harvest, (3) invest again, can also move rapidly in reverse. However, in the opposite direction it appears as (1) sell, (2) sell lower, or (3) liquidate the assets. The stock market crash of 2000–2003 was just this type of reversal of fortune.

Return without Risk: Not Bad if You Can Get It

Managers, executives, and entrepreneurs who deliver strong performance *should* collect compensation and rewards commensurate with their work. Investors providing capital to risky ventures *should* be entitled to high, risk-adjusted returns if the venture proves successful. Employees and investors who provide above-average performance or take above-average risk are *entitled* to above average compensation. Financial rewards flow to those who have earned them. Risk and return are the cornerstones of our capital markets. The presumptions of rational capital markets depend on motivated individuals attempting to maximize their investment return.

However, during the 1980s and to a greater extent during the 1990s, those in a position of influence could easily manipulate the organization to personal advantage without taking large, personal risk in the short term. If management desired organizational growth they certainly had the option to grow slowly through internal expansion (organic manner). Or, they could raise capital and acquire growth through the purchase of other companies. Whereas the first path was slow and tedious, the latter could be accomplished very fast. Moreover, for many it may have been glamorous.[7] The 1990s clearly demonstrated a go-go era.

---

7. See, for example, David Schweiger's *M&A Integration: A Framework for Executives and Managers,* (McGraw Hill, 2002). In this book the author describes the glamour in deal making (e.g., late nights with lawyers and bankers). However, he explains that most mergers fail to earn their expected value because the unglamorous job of integration is often ignored during the deal and mishandled afterward.

Want Growth? Just Acquire It

Through the 1990s, large companies were apt to grow through acquisition rather than through organic means. This is clearly illustrated in Table 3.1, which shows the rise and subsequent fall of IPOs, M&A transactions, New York Stock Exchange (NYSE) value, NASDAQ value, and Dow Jones Industrial Average (DJIA) value. Several explanations may be offered. First, the cost of debt financing was very low, coinciding with relatively strong institutional investor demand.[8] Thus, firms could acquire other firms with relatively cheap debt funding. Also, the public equity markets were very strong, creating an opportunity to issue new equity for acquisition financing. IPOs were very popular during this time period. Finally, and perhaps most important, the rising stock market inflated company values, thus enabling acquiring firms to buy more companies by employing a stock for stock

Table 3.1 Market Values in Millions

	1996	1997	1998	1999	2000	2001
Number of IPOs*	771	519	337	508	351	110
Number of M&As*	13,068	13,907	16,002	13,766	12,885	8,853
NYSE market value	$7,300	$9,413	$10,865	$12,296	$12,372	$11,714
NASDAQ market value	$1,512	$1,835	$2,589	$5,205	$3,597	$2,900
DJIA market value	$6,800	$7,800	$9,300	$11,700	$10,500	$9,870

* Only U.S. IPOs and M&As. Data provided by National Venture Capital Association and SDC Platinum (2002).

---

8. The demand for debt is inversely related to the interest rate: As demand rises, the bond price increases and the effective cost or yield declines.

swap.[9] As the stock markets continued to rise, acquiring companies were inclined to make even more acquisitions while the timing was right. The rationale among some managers was that they wanted to use their company's inflated stock price to buy up assets while the opportunity was available (i.e., before the stock price dropped and the opportunity would be lost).[10] However, one of the pitfalls of an overheated stock market includes unjustified bidding wars among potential buyers leading to the "winners curse." Those who won the bidding ultimately may have been "cursed" by paying too much. At the extreme, buyers paid billions of dollars in company stock for organizations that had no profits and in some cases no revenues.[11] During the mid-to-late 1990s, Lucent, Cisco, Nortel, and other telecom companies were among the most eager participants in the acquisition game.[12] In the years subsequent to their acquisitions they were also among the companies that experienced the largest loss in shareholder value.

At first, the stock markets didn't react very strongly to the acquisitions, but over time it became clear that many of the acquisitions were not working. Analysts usually need a couple of quarters before deciding whether or not an acquisition will lead to the hoped-for economies of scale or revenue expansion. During this time period, companies

---

9. Because stock prices were rising quickly for the acquiring firms, they would need fewer shares or a smaller percentage of their company to buy up another company using stock. Financiers refer to this situation as "reducing dilution," meaning that the ownership interest of existing shareholders will not be allocated to as many different new investors as much when the stock prices rise. Alternatively, a rising stock price also enables the buyer the opportunity to pay more for an acquisition.

10. See, for example, *Red Herring,* "Mergers and Acquisitions Insight: Big Deals Weaken Stocks" (August 2000). The article describes the displeasure among investors that "overvalued companies are using their inflated stock to not only buy, but to pay a premium to acquire other overvalued companies."

11. Lucent Technologies paid $20 billion for Ascend Communications, which had $1.1 billion in revenue and was losing money. Later, Lucent paid $4.8 billion for Chromatis, which had no revenues. They closed the company less than one year later.

12. According to *ZD Net Technology News* (August 1999), Lucent had spent over $30 billion for acquisitions in the prior three-year period.

need to sort out management changes and infrastructure adjustments. At best, a large acquisition requires six months to one year before benefits can be noticed, and many of these high-rolling acquirers were completing multiple acquisitions per quarter. Thus, sorting out the final year-to-year performance numbers was a difficult challenge. A November 1999 study by the accounting firm KPMG found that 83% of the 700 "most expensive deals" completed during the period 1996–1998 either broke even or lost money (53% lost money and 30% were considered break even). By contrast, 82% of the surveyed 107 executives from these participating firms believed that these deals were "successful." A study conducted by Booz, Allen, and Hamilton (2001) found similar results in the success and failure rate for companies that merged during the time period 1997–1998.[13] Many other academic studies also show that many mergers did not provide the intended cost savings or strategic benefit. Yet, even as evidence emerged indicating that many deals were not working as planned, individuals still pushed acquired growth initiatives forward. Why?

CEOs May Serve Themselves First

The fact that M&A deals continued despite mounting evidence that they may not have been in the best interests of corporate stakeholders at first seems counter-intuitive. But executives in larger organizations generally earn more than executives in smaller

---

13. Professor Robert Bruner summarized 130 empirical studies of M&A activity conducted between 1971–2001 in his paper "Does M&A Pay? A Survey of Evidence for the Decision Maker," University of Virginia, October 2001. In this evaluation, Professor Bruner cited the KPMG November 1999 report, as well as a 2001 Booz, Allen, and Hamilton study (among many others), which found that large mergers reduced shareholder value during the mid-to-late 1990s. His paper provides a balanced view of the evidence for other periods that had different results.

organizations.[14] Consequently, they may have economic incentive to acquire other firms and grow their own organization. Coinciding with the incentives of the acquiring executive, new research suggests that executives from the acquired firms also may have economic incentive to acquiesce to new ownership. In a study examining 40 large "mergers of equals," including companies such as Traveler's Group and Citicorp, AOL and Time Warner, Viacom and CBS, Daimler-Benz and Chrysler, Dean Witter and Morgan Stanley, and Bell and GTE, Wharton Professor J. Wulf suggested that CEOs from acquired firms may "trade away a better price for their shareholders in exchange for more job security for themselves." Thus, CEOs from both sides of the transaction might have economic incentive to complete a transaction.[15] Furthermore, much of the SEC fines issued during 2002 and 2003 (discussed earlier) address the strong conflict of interests that members of the financial community have regarding the completion of deals and dissemination of that information to the public.

Given the potential for a conflict of interest, a CEO of a large, public company needs to be careful about responsibilities to the shareholders and recognize that growth in revenues does not necessarily translate into greater shareholder return. Senior managers

---

14. See, for example, "Performance Pay and Top Management Incentive," Jensen and Murphy, *Journal of Political Economy,* 1990, Vol. 98, No. 2 or "CEO Incentives and Firm Size," Hall and Baker, Harvard Working Paper, 2002.

15. Professor Julie Wulf, Research at Penn, August 2001, "CEOs Serve Themselves First in Mergers of Equals." In her study evaluating 40 major transactions of mergers of equal size, Wulf concluded that CEOs of target companies often traded away a better price for their shareholders in exchange for more job security for themselves (or possibly their employees). "Merger agreements that appoint a larger share of target directors to the post-merger board and that include CEO/chairman succession plans are associated with lower target shareholder returns." Her study included companies such as Traveler's Group and Citicorp, AOL and Time Warner, Viacom and CBS, Daimler-Benz and Chrysler, Dean Witter and Morgan Stanley, and Bell and GTE.

can lead the firm to new heights or drive it off a cliff. Obviously, any major decision is subject to board and shareholder approval, but top managers can dictate the direction of the organization. Given their unique opportunity to shepherd resources, acquire other companies, or radically change the fabric of the entire organization, this group has power. Big power. But if they are to take advantage of their unique power they will need to move fast. Their stay at the top lasts for only a short while. Nowadays, most executives leading large, publicly held companies survive, on average, 3-4 years before they move on. In many respects, their career at the top approximates the life of a National Football League running back.[16] If they are to make significant change within the organization, or hope to make a big score in compensation, they will only have a short window of opportunity in which to accomplish it.

Management by the Numbers: Executive Compensation and Shareholder Return

The media frequently evaluates whether or not management earns its pay. Comparisons of salaries to corporate performance often appear once the latest compensation figures are made public in the spring.[17] Does extraordinary compensation correspond with high stock returns? Increasingly, the answer appears to be no. In 2002,

---

16. We searched company records of CEO duration at *Fortune* 500 companies over the time period 1995–2000 and came to an average duration of approximately four years. A study reported by East Bay Business Times (July 2002), "Revolving Doors for CEOs Turning Quicker," conducted by human resource firm DBM, evaluated 481 public and private firms in 25 countries during 2000 and 2001. They found the average duration among U.S. CEOs was only three years.

17. See, for example, "Executive Pay," *Business Week,* April 17, 2000.

three of the top six wage earners all worked for Tyco, a company that in the prior year was under intense scrutiny for corporate impropriety and greed. Despite the 22% stock market decline in 2002 for the S&P 500, the executive compensation for *Fortune* 100 executives rose 14% to $13.2 million. This has created outrage among shareholders and as one pay consultant has put it, "not only does executive pay seem more decoupled from performance than ever, but boards are conveniently changing their definition of performance." As famed investor Warren Buffet noted: the "acid test for reform will be executive compensation."[18] This suggests that going forward management actions will perhaps need to be more closely linked to total stakeholder performance.

But, compensation experts are divided on the problems related to management excess. Since greater than 90% of all executive compensation is now in the form of long-term stock options, many experts contend that the problem is self-correcting.[19] Executives don't earn benefits related to stock options unless they help the stock price rise. The argument contends that if executives earn exceptional compensation, it is only because they have lifted the stock price to which their interests are directly aligned.

There are, of course, counter-arguments that are relevant for our purposes. The first one addresses timing. If executives can "game" the stock price such that it rises high enough to exercise some of their options in the immediate term, they will gain. If, later on, the stock price ultimately plummets, they will have gained at the expense of the shareholders, though their future options may expire without value. All of this presumes that management can help influence the price movement of the stock. In actuality,

---

18. See "CEO Pay: Have They No Shame?," *Fortune*, April 13, 2003.
19. See, for example, "What You Really Need to Know about Stock Options," Hall, Harvard Business Review, March 1, 2000.

management's behavior may be completely unrelated to any stock price movement. In a strong "Bear" market, even Herculean management efforts may be insufficient to move the stock price up. Similarly, in a rising "Bull" market, the stock price may benefit irrespective of management's mistakes.

Critics maintain that stock options are best applied when they are measured or calibrated relative to some meaningful benchmark. This, they suggest, eliminates extraordinary levels of compensation for mediocre performance or uncontrolled externalities. Critics worry that compensation boards tend to be lax with their controls, and that CEOs have far more power and influence over their own salaries than they should be entitled.[20] Statistics back up the critics' claims. During the decade 1990–2000, CEO compensation increased by an average of 1,300% compared to the average employee salary increase of 43%.[21] Moreover, the gap between U.S. and international CEO pay continues to widen.

Aside from the question of whether such a differential is appropriate, there are other questions concerning the market's response.[22] Can executives who reap these enormous financial rewards keep their companies going strong? The data suggests that they can't. Further, the most highly compensated executives tend to pursue above-average M&A activity. Some executives may be using transaction activity to demonstrate growth and help justify their

---

20. See "CEO Pay: Have They No Shame?," *Fortune*, April 13, 2003.
21. Executive Pay: The Great CEO Pay Heist," *Fortune* magazine, June 11, 2001. See also, "Are CEOs Really Paid Like Bureaucrats?," Hall and Liebman, *NBER*, August, 1998.
22. As an interesting sidebar, Executive Pay watchdogs are becoming more vigilant and organized in their monitoring behavior. For example, in 2003, Executive Pay-Watch organized by the AFL–CIO, is monitoring 16 *Fortune* 500 companies being targeted for "extraordinary executive pension cases." To the extent that these efforts become more widely disseminated, they may help stem the gap between the average worker and executive officer.

salaries for personal benefit. Future growth models need to ensure that the interests of all stakeholders are more closely aligned for both short- and long-term considerations.

Highest Paid = Highest Performance? A Look at *Business Week*'s Top 20

Business Week's most highly compensated executives include some of the most closely monitored individuals at some of the most celebrated organizations. It is almost a mathematical certainty that in order to make *Business Week*'s Top 20 Compensation list, the stock had to rise precipitously over the prior period. In some situations, the high compensation represented one terrific year for the company, whereas in other situations the high compensation represented an executive selling a lifetime's accumulation of stock options. Either way it is interesting to assess how the stock performed in the periods *after* the executive harvested his options.[23] The data generally show that the more highly compensated CEOs had more revenue growth with their companies and considerably higher M&A activity (up to 4 times greater) compared to similar companies in the same industry! Moreover, the stock of highly compensated CEOs generally performed worse than the S&P 500 (benchmark index) in the periods after the CEO harvested his stock options. Furthermore, the evidence suggests that on average, if a highly paid executive is in office for more than 10 years (i.e., well-entrenched executive), the executives are more likely to under-perform the industry benchmark after cashing out of stock options. The exceptions to this rule were Jack Welch at General Electric and company founders (e.g., Andy Grove at Intel, Bill Gates at Microsoft, Larry Ellison at Oracle, and Michael Dell at Dell Computers) that continued to outperform the market.[24] Consequently, in the years before the executives cashed out of their stock options, their companies had more M&A activity (on average); in the years after they cashed out, their company stocks (on average) performed poorly. Clearly, future models of growth would benefit by examining potential long-term growth and compensation developments.

CEO Influence: Examples of Style

If, in fact, M&A activity is related to poor subsequent stock performance, executives should seek fewer deals than they do. More important, it is counter-intuitive that executives get financially rewarded for pursuing transactions that *in the long run* reduce stakeholder value. In a few high-profile transactions like,

---

23. We examined the potential for CEO influence on stock returns and organizational growth. In particular, we searched our *Fortune* 500 database for highly compensated executives to determine whether or not a relationship existed between individual compensation incentives and organizational growth. In determining our list of highly compensated executives, we ranked the top 20 most highly compensated executives provided by COMPUSTATs EXECUCOMP database (also listed in *Business Week* and *The Wall Street Journal*) for the period 1993–2000 and compared the results for organizational revenue growth, stock price appreciation, and subsequent performance. Invariably, in order for the executives to be listed on the most highly compensated list, it was necessary for the stock to perform well preceding the executive's sale of stock options. This was the case in every situation because company stock options comprised the bulk of executive compensation. The bigger question was, What was the stock performance like after the executive sold his stock?

We were also interested in the type of growth that occurred with high compensation, so we searched the Securities Data Corp. (SDC) for M&A activity. In each case we compared the M&A activity of companies in our sample (i.e., those representing highly compensated CEOs) with other companies in the same respective industry peer group.

for example, Travelers Group and Citigroup, senior executives sold their firms to rivals, pocketing an enormous windfall as they walked away.[25] Many subordinates would be later fired or pushed out in the consolidation and often the combined entity would not reap the projected advantages of synergy. Given these obvious potential conflicts of interest, shouldn't compensation programs address these potentially disastrous developments?

Lessons Learned?

Poorly designed organizational compensation incentives are largely to blame for the problems experienced through much of the 1990s.[26] Many of the individuals who were listed among *Business Week's* top paid executives were among our list of fastest revenue-growing firms during the same time period (or were involved in

---

24. We also found other interesting relationships regarding the variance of executive compensation and stock performance. We found a modest relationship between the variance between the top two executives and stock performance. For example, in the case of General Electric, our top-performing company, the CEO consistently earned between 1.8 and 2.2 times more than the second-in-command. By contrast, at Disney, a company whose stock returns lagged that of many others in our database, the CEO in some years earned up to 50 times the amount of the second-in-command. Although the data are inconclusive regarding this statistic, we would expect that the company culture would be appreciably different at the two companies. Also, we found that bringing together two members of the *Business Week* highly compensated list into one team was detrimental for stockholders (AOL and Time/Warner merger). More insights are available at Executive Compensation and Stock Returns, Joel Shulman working paper, with the guidance of Brian Hall, Harvard Business School, 2000.

25. Professor Julie Wulf, Research at Penn, August 2001, "CEOs Serve Themselves First in Mergers of Equals." Her study included companies such as Traveler's Group and Citicorp, AOL and Time Warner, Viacom and CBS, Daimler-Benz and Chrysler, Dean Witter and Morgan Stanley, and Bell and GTE.

26. In his June 9, 2002 article, "Heads I Win, Tails I Win," *The New York Times,* Lowenstein cited an example of how a CEO (Edward Whitacre) at SBC earned $82 million for a very mediocre performance.

management impropriety). However, revenue growth (particularly growth gained through acquisition) did not lead to strong stockholder performance. Because acquired growth can accomplish an organizational overhaul very quickly, it is probably not surprising that this methodology has been subject to abuse. Ultimately, the shareholders lost, despite management's predictions that their organization might perform well with the acquired assets.[27]

Although acquired growth may not benefit shareholder wealth creation, it offers a path for senior management to create personal wealth. And, the bias toward creating deals may result, in part, from the short duration of CEO tenure. Given their relatively short stay at the top (i.e., three to four years), CEOs have great incentive to promote M&A activity or other transactions that will foster growth, facilitate a culture change, or manipulate a stock option harvest. Furthermore, given the large wealth transfer with M&A activity, many deals may also have been driven by pressures from investment bankers, venture capitalists, lawyers, and other financial advisors who would substantially gain from the harvest.

Do Senior Agents Represent Themselves More than Other Stakeholders?

Clearly, growth through acquisition was not the best path to increasing shareholder return, yet acquisitions continued at an aggressive pace for over a decade. This appears to be a problem of "Agency Costs" when agents for the firm consume corporate

---

27. See KPMG, November 1999 study of merger activity on 700 large transactions between 1996–1998. Although 83% of the 700 M&As evaluated during the time period either performed poorly or broke even, 82% of the executives involved in the transaction described them as "successful."

perquisites at the expense of other stakeholders.[28] For example, managers may choose to fly first class or pay themselves large bonuses. Other agents, such as investment bankers, may drive deals to generate fees irrespective of whether value is created for their clients. In the case of the Daimler Chrysler merger, Goldman Sachs received a reported $65 million in fees, whereas CS First Boston received approximately $55 million.[29] Other examples may include management that chooses to acquire companies for personal benefit. Management at the acquired firm often gets fired as part of the cost reductions with a horizontal (similar industry) consolidation. Thus, completely independent of cost savings or market share issues, management from the acquiring firm may believe that there is job security, as well as personal financial gain, to be found in buying other organizations.

Incentive Orientation: Things Need to Change

What methods can successfully grow an organization if the leaders of the entity are gaming the system for personal benefit? Before stock options became popular in the 1980s, executives focused on corporate perquisites, a nice salary, and respect among peers and coworkers. Things were simpler and more predictable in the past. In our newer economy, time in the job has shortened and the rules of engagement are different. Most of an executive's compensation and wealth creation now comes from stock appreciation. Thus

---

28. For a discussion of agency costs, see "Theory of the Firm: Managerial Behavior, Agency Costs, and Ownership Structure," Jensen and Meckling, *Journal of Financial Economics,* October, 1976, Vol. 3, No. 4.
29. Levy Zuckerman, "Merger Mayhem," *Bloomberg Magazine*, October 1998.

management has incentive to push the stock price higher, even for just a little while.[30] However, management becomes dependent on the marketplace to recognize value in their collective efforts. If the entire market drifts down, or their efforts are not recognized as valuable, then no matter how hard they work, their large rewards will not be recognized.

Considerable time and attention are placed on the company's stock price. Management is under great pressure to push the price higher. Yet management does not have much time. Thus, it has become the norm in many cases for management to expend great efforts to boost the price up quickly. Mergers, divestitures, refinancings, equity carve-outs, venture funds, extensive layoffs and cost-cutting, strategic alliances, and so forth, are all considered for the sake of expanding corporate revenues and profits. The status quo is not an attractive option, nor is slow growth.

As discussed in Chapter 5, the best growth comes about through strategic expansion and organic growth. Growth through acquisition does not contribute to good stock performance though growth through organic means (i.e., internal expansion) contributes to strong stock performance. It may take longer and may not push revenues soaring as quickly as acquired growth, but it has a stronger impact on the stock price in the long term.

More of the incentive structure should be focused on creating organic growth rather than growth through acquired means. Compensation mechanisms in many firms have become short-

---

30. Actually, the wealth creation comes from stock options (in a rising stock market) with salary and bonus providing a floor. Individuals closely monitor the stock option exercise price or strike price (the point where they can buy the stock) and have incentive to push the market price above this level. Because stock options enable great return for relatively small price movements, they can create much greater wealth accumulation in a shorter period of time compared to the outright stock purchase.

term-oriented with managers being concerned about immediate shareholder gratification. Organizations need to do a better job of tracking performance based on the value added by key talent.

During the 1990s, corporate behavior entered a new arena that has since become scrutinized and criticized. The markets are now ready for a change in corporate compensation. Shareholders, regulators, government officials, and employees are demanding change now. Executives at major organizations are now being more heavily scrutinized in regard to their compensation. Board members are being more closely monitored too.

In Chapter 7 you consider modifications to the existing incentive structure. The changes are not meant for the entire organization, but rather, a small element that can be affiliated with the parent. If successful, the approach might become influential on the parent, but changing the culture of the parent is an extraordinarily complex task beyond the scope of this text. Furthermore, much of the discussion in this chapter focused on the behavior of senior management. As you explore in the next chapter it is unfair to place the burden solely on the shoulders of senior management and their advisors. In the past 20 to 30 years, middle management has been the cause of some large-organization decay as well. In the next chapter you look at how large organizations might be better able to utilize their human capital in the middle. Then, in subsequent chapters you consider modifications to existing compensation structures in which all employees might be able to work together to help create long-term value for their stakeholders.

4

RESISTANCE TO CHANGE—WAYS TO LEVERAGE THE CONCRETE MIDDLE

Although CEO compensation may have produced undesirable behaviors during the late 1990s, as mentioned in the previous chapter, the resistance of middle management to change, or the inability to challenge the status quo, equally hampered the long-term success of many firms. The tendency of corporate managers to build in a conservative bias against new ways of doing business or expansion is well known. This tendency is so strong that it hampers new ventures and is one reason that the SEU model may encourage growth by isolating the new idea from the old hard-line bureaucratic management. This chapter will describe the problem and why the SEU model can also be used to help change the established firm.

Just Do It My Way and Don't Ask Questions

As firms grow along the life cycle curve toward maturity, functional specialization necessarily develops with the company. Although small start-ups can have multitasked managers handling several different assignments, larger firms create specific departments to bring expertise to functions like Human Resources, Procurement, Marketing, and Sales. It's actually not a bad thing and permits the company to grow by letting these staff activities standardize the way the company operates. It may be fashionable to look down on these functional experts, but without them the firm would be a chaotic mess of disjointed approaches. It is this standardization of procedures and policies that actually allows firms to expand into new areas and still have some type of control and consistency.

The danger in establishing these departmental experts is that they can become tiny (or sometime large) empires of their own and can begin to segment the company into silos or separate areas. The professional manager may bring expertise but he may also see that his power and authority comes from not allowing deviation to his policies. How many times have we heard the expression, "That's the way Human Resources says it has to be done," or "Systems won't approve your request," or the all-time favorite, "That's just the way we do it here." The institutionalized response keeps things in line and may be efficient, but it can also hamper creativity and stifle new ideas.

Inbred Management at Ford Purchasing

Hiding behind the authority of specialized expertise, these functional departments are often large enough to create career paths solely within their own area. Prior to recent changes, the Ford Motor Company had a large procurement function that coordinated its world-wide buying functions for almost 40 years. It was a model of efficiency and many consultants thought Ford's expertise was the best in the industry. Ford Supply had its own recruitment and training area and its own Human Resources function and management development roles. Many of its employees were hired into Ford Procurement and Supply and spent their entire careers in the same function, moving along the many rungs of its management. Until the current Vice President, Tony Brown, was brought in from United Technologies, every previous VP of Procurement at Ford had grown up entirely within that area without any cross-functional assignments to other areas like engineering, manufacturing, or sales. Promotions were made based on how well the subordinate followed the rules and managers picked their successors from among those who acted and thought just like them. It became a very inbred system that faced off against similar internal silos (compartmentalized divisions from which information does not readily flow back and forth to other parts of the company) like engineering. By the late 1990s, members of Ford's management team were locked in turf battles protecting their own areas instead of working on joint solutions. Many people who have looked at the previous Ford structure have complained that this institutional inbreeding resulted in a management that could not operate as a team and infected the culture of the company by resisting the necessary changes that are only now occurring under the new management of Bill Ford.

Clearly, this Ford example is not unique. Most big companies have created internal departments that are inbred, isolated, and separated from the rest of the company. Often, these departments seemingly work well and help keep the firm from bogging down as it expands. A common problem, however, is that this type of organization also rewards those who keep their head down, don't make waves, and measure their productivity by the speed with which they process the mail in their in-basket. The comparison to the old WWII military hierarchy is not entirely incorrect. Although most businessmen laugh at the hide-bound image of the military, there is in fact little difference between the way middle managers respond in a big corporate bureaucracy and the way first line officers conduct their commands in the military. Now both types of groups are trying to change their respective organizations and free up middle management.

The Problem of the Concrete Middle

It is only natural that even though these strong and separate functional departments were created for a good purpose, another not so beneficial practice would result. People mimic successful people, organizations mimic other companies, and managers copy others that seem to be in vogue. As a result of internally biased promotional avenues, these strong departments created a unique culture of conformity and rigid resistance to change. Because promotion and merit increases were based on following the status quo, middle management gradually become entrenched in the system and instead of modifying it, they become the strongest internal advocates to avoid change instead of embracing it.

Part of the problem comes from the incentive compensation method that rewards conformity, but more comes from the power of the rules of authority that conformity brings. If you are the person in charge of a department with sole administrative control over an area, you have a great deal of very real power. Resisting changes to that authority and policing that consistency becomes the most important task for such a person. An ironic example comes from the days of the merger of Daimler Benz and Chrysler.

Daimler is an old company; it invented the car over 110 years ago. Through those years, Daimler survived two world wars (on the losing end both times), several economic disasters, and multiple reorganizations. Although the company changed formats, it remained an extremely structured and bureaucratic organization. In the planning phase to announce what was, up to that time, the world's largest industrial merger, both the Chrysler and Daimler public relations (PR) departments worked to come up with a program worthy of the historic occasion. It was decided that the first day of listing the global shares of DCX on the NYSE would be the appropriate setting for this extravaganza. The two separate PR departments set out to decide the suitable commemorative gift for the press, analysts, and dignitaries who would attend the opening at the stock exchange.

It quickly became apparent to the Chrysler side that they were up against a strong opposing force in the Daimler PR department. Chrysler insisted on absolute control over virtually all aspects of the gift, including packaging. Daimler, on the other hand, announced that it maintained inside its Corporate Identity department a group responsible solely for the approval of boxes used for company gifts. They had a manual of guidelines that clearly spelled out the color, texture, and material to be used in all packages related to the Mercedes brand. They refused to relinquish their standards for this first gift from the new company that was to be created from the two merged companies. The result was the standard blue corrugated paper box that was used for all Mercedes events. It was tasteful and classy but was viewed by the Chrysler side, which wanted something more contemporary, as old-fashioned and not something to showcase the "Deal of the Century." A giant controversy arose out of what should have been a simple thing.

Through their informal and historic formal authority, the Daimler side forced their decision on the Chrysler side. The commemorative Swatch watch contained in the gift box had a band that when opened spelled out the name of the new company, DaimlerChrylser. Although this design was approved by both sides, it was a telling sign that when the watch was place on the wrist, the Chrysler brand name was overlapped and hidden underneath the Daimler name—an omen of things to come and a disappointment to all on the Chrysler side.

Although this may seem to be a petty example of internal middle management resistance, it highlights how strongly existing managers will fight for what they think is the preservation of their beliefs or against what they perceive as a potential threat to their jobs. This solid immovable group has been appropriately called the Concrete Middle layer of management.

The Concrete Middle is an unintended consequence of the hierarchy of companies. Middle management actually runs the organization by the nature of their jobs and has much more influence that is readily apparent on an organization chart. They see themselves as protectors of the Corporate History and often are more permanent in their tenure than the CEOs who come in through the revolving door at the top. The Concrete Middle is the layer that must be worked through to implement change and in many cases they can resist even the strongest efforts. They represent the culture of the company and must be considered in any plan to challenge the historical way of running the firm.

An Organized Resistance Campaign

A great example of the power of the Concrete Middle is the resistance to change at Chrysler after the acquisition of American

Motors in 1987 (AMC). For over a decade, AMC had been operating on a very thin R&D budget compared to Chrysler and the other Big Three, but it still had been able to turn out a surprising number of new models in both car categories and what was the beginning of the SUV categories. Constant profit improvement campaigns had reduced the AMC corporate staff to a bare minimum and many functions had been outsourced from the company to reduce overhead. As a result, many departments performed dual or triple functions, which created an extremely lean and fast organization. They produced new models faster, cheaper, and with less investment than any other domestic manufacturers. In fact, AMC turned out nearly as many models as Chrysler with only 20% of the engineering staff. Its only major problem was the quality level, which was significantly below any of the others.

It was apparent to many within Chrysler that a "reverse merger" in culture was necessary. Instead of integrating AMC into the Chrysler structure, Bob Lutz and Francois Castaing (from AMC) conceived the idea to integrate Chrysler into the AMC model and led a major overhaul of the whole Chrysler organization. Castaing, who was originally from Renault, replaced Chrysler's well-respected head of engineering. This change did not sit well with the large and entrenched Chrysler engineering workforce. They considered it an insult that someone from outside (especially from Renault) was picked to run their organization, which had prided itself on internal development. Chrysler Engineers had a long history of invention and were well-regarded in the industry. They even ran their own Institute that granted Masters level degrees to junior engineers as they worked their way up the predicted rungs of the ladder of promotion.

Upon learning of the replacement of their leader, the Engineering middle management conducted a fierce letter-writing campaign to the then-Chairman of Chrysler, Lee Iacocca, who was

tempted to back down by the threats of revolt. In the end, Bob
Lutz convinced Iacocca to stick with his decision but not after
weeks of tension and turmoil inside the company. The middle
management tried to exert its informal authority and, fortunately
for the future of the company, they lost. Castaing became one of a
team of senior managers who led the transition from the silo structure to a cross-functional product development team approach. It
was this pivotal situation that helped change the orientation from
an individual to team approach that led Chrysler to be the most
profitable car company, on a per-unit basis, in the 1990s. If
Iacocca had given in to the Concrete Middle, the company would
not have become the success that made it an attractive merger candidate with Daimler Benz.

Problems with Culture:
The Case at Chrysler/Daimler

In many instances, M&As have a public posture to justify the deal
and an internal situation that are often in conflict. Certainly the
publicity, turmoil, and lack of financial accomplishments in the
merger of Chrysler and Daimler Benz highlight this situation to an
extreme. Three years after the highly publicized deal, touted as the
biggest and best "Merger of Equals" in the manufacturing world,
results have been less than spectacular, both managerially and
financially. Senior management from Chrysler has been replaced,
shareholder value has declined from a stock price of $100 per share
in 1999 to $44 per share in 2002, and thousands of other workers
have been "restructured" out of a job as the new company tries to
respond to competitive pressures to cut costs.

Why was this merger so unsuccessful? There were two major reasons: the vastly different corporate culture at each organization and the failure to agree on the power and authority base after the merger.

The culture issues grounded themselves in the very existence of each individual corporation. Daimler, for example, had its roots going back to the late 1890s and could creditably lay claim to having invented the automobile, if not once but twice, because both Gottleib Daimler and Carl Benz independently produced early models within months of each other in Germany. Daimler, operating as a German AG, was structured into 22 separate business units, making such diverse products as trains, aerospace components, heavy trucks, luxury automobiles, and purely financial institutions. Each business unit had its own management team and operated as a separate profit and loss center, including R&D units.

Chrysler, however, was a relative upstart, having been formed in the United States in the 1920s by an executive from General Motors as a manufacturer of cars and light trucks. They were very centralized with no profit and loss responsibility, other than at corporate level. All units were treated as cost centers and the management group operated as a team. During its famous turnaround in the late 1990s, the management team, lead by then-President Bob Lutz, established a reputation as fast, loose, and decisive. The business press named them the "Dream Team" and *Forbes* made Chrysler their Company of the Year in 1998. It was that public recognition and financial success that made them a prime candidate for a merger with Daimler.

Unfortunately, the radically different cultures were overlooked or discounted during the negotiations. Early attempts at combining elements of the automotive units were resisted as being potentially confusing to the brand image and to customers. Projects to combine back offices and nonvisible areas were also slow to gather momentum and the synergistic savings failed to materialize.

However, the different power and authority structure was the larger roadblock to the merger. The Daimler structure was extremely rigid and hierarchical, whereas Chrysler was less formal. Within Chrysler, senior management bounced decisions off of one another to arrive at consensus, or at least agreement. Daimler's many units operated independently with little internal discussion, other than through financial reports.

It was determined that the new, combined entity would follow the existing legal structure of a German corporation for tax and shareholder purposes. It operated with a Management Board consisting of 17 senior executives (8 from the American Chrysler side and 9 from the German Daimler side) and met weekly to review the financial and strategic decisions for the firm. These sessions were extremely formal with pre-negotiated set agendas, detailed financial presentations, and a limited exchange of ideas or thoughts. From the first meeting, it became clear that the challenging and open "face-to-face" style of Chrysler was at odds with the formal, "don't ask if it's not your business" style of Daimler.

The atmosphere in these sessions was tense as the Chrysler members adjusted to the rigidity of the meetings and the Daimler side reeled from the Chrysler executive's constant questioning about the financial reporting. One example was the mind-numbing three meetings it took to produce a detailed cash forecast, something Daimler never had previously done for the Board. Because the arguments and questions got to be so divisive, the subject was declared closed, rather than working through for a resolution. These problems led to the formation of an Executive Group responsible for making the actual decisions and reporting to the

Board. Obviously, this created two levels of executives, and increased tension rather than reducing it.

The resolution of such cultural and power differences was simple yet drastic. Within a period of 11 months, the Chrysler management team was retired, fired, or otherwise removed from the Board. As of 2002, there were only two original Chrysler members remaining on the Board and no new individuals were added from the U.S. side. The acquiring company prevailed in the long run and the experiment for a merger did not last a year. In the end, power and authority went to the company who paid for the acquisition.

A Question of Culture

As the prior case with Chrysler/Daimler indicates, differing corporate cultures can make a big difference in the manner in which a company operates. Corporate culture represents the set of values, ethics, and experiences that set the overall tone for the organization. It resides in every organization whether expressed, recognized, or cultivated. High-performing organizations recognize the need to build on a successful corporate culture to form a higher bond between employees and management. Given the ideal conditions, individuals work together toward a common goal without the need for clarification or change in direction.

Sometimes, however, the corporate culture works against general organizational goals and hurts the efficiency of operations. Rather than encourage a supportive, nurturing environment, the corporate culture may create divisive, political infighting. In these situations, management often fails to recognize that existing corporate culture can result in lost opportunities for the organization and truncated career paths for the individual.

The key is to recognize the existence of the Concrete Middle and to free them up to become agents of change. This may seem to be a paradox but that is the challenge of running a company. The middle management of a company is its productive lifeblood and it keeps the place on an even keel. It makes sure the work gets accomplished in an orderly manner. In doing so, it defines and maintains the nature of the corporation. Using start-up ventures can move a company along the growth curve and maintain its edge. But, if not considered in their formation, the Concrete Middle can kill a project or idea before it gets off the ground.

By using their control and insistence on corporate policy, the functional middle management may force the new venture to add unnecessary costs or structure. Unless the senior management really wants to tackle the resistance, like Iacocca did in the aforementioned example, the SEU concept provides an additional, perhaps easier approach.

Using the SEU to Overcome the Concrete Middle

The formation of new units or enterprises within a company provides an opportunity for the established internal organization to attempt to spread its sphere of influence. Unless considered in advance, this natural resistance can unnecessarily burden or tax the new venture from its beginning. The senior management responsible for creating and approving a new venture must act firmly to minimize this potential threat. Managers are often too removed from the working and internal politics of these functional departments to recognize the power play that is being laid upon the venture.

To merely let Human Resources, Accounting, Payroll, or other internal departments provide services to the new venture may be naïve. Because staff areas are operating as cost centers, their tendency is to use the new venture as a dumping ground for allocation charges and costs that may be too high or unnecessary.

An alternative is to form a separate SEU that operates at arm's length from the parent and is given the freedom to decide how slim its own structure should be. Particularly in the formation stages, the use of high-powered services from the "mother ship" may not be required or wanted. The SEU should be provided the opportunity to quote the parent firm for services but should also be encouraged to look for alternative ways to get these services performed.

Instead of using the elaborate Payroll system of the parent, maybe the SEU should outsource that activity to one of the many outside business services providers that exist. The internal function may strongly resist this "going outside" but it should be encouraged because it has two results: first, it avoids the excuse of the venture that they can't control their costs if services are mandated by the parent, and second, it may highlight that there are alternative approaches to the parent's legacy systems.

This process of permitting independence can be beneficial to the parent company. The SEUs can be used as experimental proving grounds for new organizational structures that may be too risky to introduce into the main company. They can provide valid evidence that changes made to the existing system will not have the dire consequences often predicted by the functional department heads of the larger company. When used as learning labs, SEUs can provide a dual function. They can permit a new venture to grow and experiment without endangering the parent firm and they can begin to provide ways of getting through resistance and objections of the Concrete Middle.

Using SEUs to introduce change back into the larger, more established firms is one of the attractive features that we believe warrants its use. The trick will be to have an enlightened senior management that recognizes this secondary purpose and promotes it without being overly protective. The SEU may sink or swim based on its own business success, but the non-financial advantages of using it as an avenue of change are enormous.

5

GROWTH MODELS NEED TO CHANGE

The Race for Corporate Growth

The race for corporate growth appears daily in the press.[1] Growth *seems* to be a good thing. But is it really, and if so, which kind of growth is the best? There are so many lists and rankings now available, it's really tough to choose. *Fortune* magazine ranks companies based on total revenues and percentage change. *Business Week* lists executives based on total compensation. *Forbes* magazine

---

1. See, for example, "Top Performers," or "100 Fastest Growing Companies: Rapid Growth in Tough Times," *Fortune*, www.fortune.com, 2003.

identifies the planet's wealthiest individuals. *The Wall Street Journal* publishes its annual rankings of strongest and weakest stock performers. And this is just the start of some of the better known lists and rankings. In our modern society, we're literally inundated with lists, rankings, scorecards, opinions, and data. Good analysts know that if anything, we usually have too much data (fraudulent situations aside)! Perhaps it's no wonder that stocks have so much volatility. Even the financial experts can't agree on how to value assets and which data to watch.

Which are the key items for investors and managers to monitor? Should you monitor assets? Revenues? Net income? Corporate net worth? How influential are CEOs to stock performance? In the past few years, we've read about massive, newsworthy deals. Lots of people including management, shareholders, and employees get swept up in the news and big transactions. But do these data relate to stock performance and do they create value for the company's other stakeholders?

Just because a company or executive makes the evening news or front page of a key business periodical does not mean that this company or individual is necessarily better than any other. For example, executives making *Business Week*'s most highly compensated list are not necessarily more deserving or better than their peers. Perhaps these individuals were simply blessed with good timing or circumstances. Moreover, it's quite possible that their large payday comes at the end of a relatively long, successful career and they simply saved all of their accumulated stock to the end. So what? High pay does not by itself suggest strong performance. Similarly, the fascination with gargantuan M&As does not necessarily state that these combinations are either good for the combined entity or create value for the stakeholders. In fact, they may just be newsworthy because of the size and influence of the deal in the community. They may be in the press because a lot of people will lose their jobs with the consolidation.

Informed stakeholders, including common stock shareholders and creditors, need to see through all the information releases and determine which events and behavior are good for the company and which are not. But it's not always easy and conflicting signals abound. High executive compensation does not necessarily correspond with strong talent and high future performance. Also, strong revenue growth does not imply continued growth in revenues or profits. Such is the situation in today's marketplace. Investors need to learn the rules as they go along. Unfortunately, some investors are now learning this lesson the hard way—after they have already lost most of their gains from the 1990s.

To be sure, investors and managers prefer some growth to the alternative of no growth. Why not? More growth is always better, isn't it? Clearly, maintaining operations with no growth is not desirable. Rarely (except in an overall declining environment or improving margin situation) do you read about executives or shareholders boasting about an organization shrinking in size. But, extraordinary growth may not be good for investors or employees. In fact, it may be very bad. Often two large companies, such as AOL and Time Warner, come together and create a lousy combination. Political infighting, lost opportunities, redundant costs, and expensive severance packages all contribute to large inefficiencies in the short term. Thus, you are left with several conundrums. For example, growth generally is good, but high growth may not be good. Or, you may discover that no growth is bad, but high growth might be bad too. Finally, you have the possibility that no growth is bad and high growth may be good or bad.

These outcomes create difficult choices. Sometimes evaluating management decisions and internal and external reactions can be very complex. As you consider later, it is quite possible that growth should not be uniformly defined as good or bad; it just depends on the stakeholders' relationship to the organization and the type of risk–return tradeoff in consideration. Although this simple resolution does not sweep all problems under the rug, there is a different mechanism to evaluate growth. It may not be universal in application and perfect in prediction, but it offers external parties a more accurate reading on where the company is headed. Moreover, it offers management a better yardstick to measure their true contributions.

All Growth Is Not Equal

All growth is not equally desirable to all stakeholders of the organization. For example, some managers, perhaps induced by dreams of fame and fortune, may be biased to grow the firm in size despite knowing that it does not reward other stakeholders (i.e., equity shareholders). Shareholders, on the other hand, would like to see the stock price rise irrespective of sales growth, asset growth, or individual compensation. But who decides growth and how can patterns be changed?

Much of what management does on a daily basis is not necessarily a manifestation of individual decision making or organizational renegades, but rather an extension of corporate culture. To be sure, on the margin, individuals may take advantage of opportunities within a flawed system. But the inherent gridlock in organizational processes and the narrow pursuit of basic patterns with the Concrete Middle largely reflects institutional habit and societal norms.[2] This is a major problem that executives of large orga-

---

2. The Concrete Middle was referenced in the last chapter as the corporate gridlock among middle managers that do not have economic incentive to push the company forward in an aggressive manner.

nizations acknowledge, but unfortunately cannot easily change or modify. These corporate culture habits are embedded in the organizational fiber and take years to develop. In the absence of radical change or corporate upheaval, there is little incentive or momentum to do anything different. Consequently, old rules support unimaginative, bureaucratic behavior among middle and upper management. After a while this orientation becomes detrimental to all stakeholders.

There exists a method of growth that provides superior returns to long-term shareholders. But it runs counter to the incentive clauses currently in place. It requires a new model for organizational growth that may threaten some managers who are comfortable in a bureaucratic environment. Those members who choose to follow this different method will undoubtedly sense some risk to their career. After all, they will be pursuing a brave new vision that is still being tested. But if it works, they have the potential for pushing their personal careers and organizations to new heights. Furthermore, if handled in the context of a portfolio of small investments, the risk and cost structure to the firm is actually very low. The actual costs and risk to the firm for managing new growth may even be lower than the firm's current situation.

High Growth: Does It Guarantee Fame and Fortune?

During the 1990s, WorldCom and MCI combined in a massive merger suggesting to shareholders that there would be strong growth in corporate assets (compared to the prior period) and improved efficiency. Yet this merger, not unlike other major mergers (such as Chrysler/Daimler), ultimately resulted in smaller combined revenues and assets in periods subsequent to the consolidation.[3] Other companies, such as Enron and Tyco, boasted explosive sales growth using other innovative (later determined to be inappropriate) techniques. WorldCom, Enron, and Tyco demonstrate how management impropriety and manipulation pushed the company higher to meet external expectations. Unfortunately, no one can know now, and will probably never know, how many other companies were misdirected as a result of management impropriety, although investors are now becoming more vigilant in their evaluations. Ultimately, the markets discovered that the extraordinary revenue growth for WorldCom, Tyco, and Enron did not create true value for shareholders. Improper accounting entries and other inappropriate management behavior contributed to each entity's decline. But what can be known about the incentives for different stakeholders that were built into the growth plan for each of these companies? Isn't it possible that the incentives are similar at other companies and maybe no one there has uncovered all of the problems yet? For example, in 2002–2003 a number of firms in the financial industry were rocked by a massive $1.335 billion collective total of penalties for inappropriate business practices. Isn't it possible that this sort of behavior also occurs at other companies that have thus far eluded detection?

There are plenty of other case scenarios, discussed later, that also did not work out for shareholders. To be sure, we are not just referring to major corporate scandal or illegal behavior. There are

---

3. For example, using popular press ranking criteria, for largest absolute increase in revenue growth, the 1999–2000 "winner" was Exxon with a 63% increase in revenues to $164 billion. However, these statistics may be a little misleading. After adjusting for the merger with Mobil, and recognizing that the *combined* entities actually had a decline in revenue of $14 billion from 1997 to 1999 along with a decline in number of employees from 114,000 to 107,000, it's likely that perhaps some other company or companies might be more appropriately labeled "best growth."

lots of situations in which managers and key consultants/advisors/ financiers did more for themselves than for shareholders, though did nothing illegal. These individuals often have an inherent, economic bias to focus more on growth in revenues and assets than shareholder returns in the *short term*. Simply stated, senior executives and their advisors (*especially* their advisors) may be able to benefit at the expense of shareholders. These individuals receive greater annual compensation, bonuses, and fee income. However, there is no question that executives would also like to see the stock rise. Because most of their compensation ultimately rests with stock options, they have a clear incentive to promote stock growth.

But there is a *timing* issue that is very much in their control. If the market is hot and financing is cheap, then it becomes easy for managers to buy companies in the short term. As long as the stock price in the near term does not dip (which may happen in a hyperactive market), then even M&As about which dealmakers and decisions are uncertain (i.e., unsure whether or not they make sense in the long term) will be pursued due to short-term benefits.[4] Further, each of the key (i.e., influential) advisors/consultants/financiers/venture capitalists generates significant fee income with the closing of a deal. Many of these people had personal incentive to complete deals—even if they knew that it might be bad for the company and many of its stakeholders long term.

---

4. In other words, if the stock position is presumed to remain neutral in the short term (or possibly rise with a rising stock market) then even bad deals become a riskless situation in the short term and may provide an option for long-term wealth later on (if participants are ultimately successful in squeezing economies of scale from the combination). Moreover, the excitement generated from a "good combination" may provide a short-term blip in the stock market, creating great value in existing stock options. Thus, executive compensation may benefit with stock options already "in-the-money" and may be able to improve their base pay (because executives at larger companies tend to earn more) at the same time.

Career Paths on the Fly: Action = Money

Estimates suggest that as many as 5000 high-tech millionaires were created each *month* during the "gold-rush" days of 1999–2000. Such wealth creation was largely credited to successful IPOs or company harvests through sale. Back in 1998–2000, it was relatively easy to make big money. Soaring stock prices inflated IPO values, which were then used as currency to buy other companies at high prices. By way of example, the total dollar value of shares traded on the NASDAQ Stock Market during the first half of 2000 climbed to $10.8 trillion. This was an increase of 125% from the prior year and appreciably higher than a few years before. With this surge of wealth, many companies bought other companies pushing their collective, inflated values higher and higher. However this IPO and acquisition ploy changed in the year 2000. By 2001, over 300 dot.coms filed for bankruptcy and more were planning the same. The high-flying NASDAQ index was down over 40% (causing several trillion dollars in lost investor wealth) and both IPO and M&A transactions came to a near halt. Such was the drastic turnaround from the heady days in the late 1990s. Investors learned that money could be made quickly and could be lost just as fast. But these were special times and most participants involved in the deals knew it.

People behind the deals were savvy enough to know that they had to work fast or forever lose their once-in-a-lifetime opportunity. High growth was the "play" and acquisitions or IPOs were the vehicles of choice. Cheap financing and creative dealmakers took care of the rest. It was all about the money. Consider the following situations. In 1999, prestigious investment banking firms (i.e., Goldman Sachs, etc.) would go to Harvard Business School (among other leading graduate programs) and not fill their interview schedule. Why?

Approximately 35 to 40% of the graduating class shunned the traditional career path of Wall Street and consulting (such as McKinsey or Bain) to pursue their dream in dot.com start-ups. Another 25 to 30% attempted to move into the lucrative VC or private equity markets. Yes, these were unusual years. Even experienced executives took unusual risks and strayed away from their safe career path. It actually became commonplace for executives from large companies to leave their secure, high-paying salaries in pursuit of a start-up venture. To be certain, their dream included entrepreneurial excitement, growth, recognition, opportunity, and a chance to make a difference on a winning team. Let's not forget an important, driving factor. They also pursued money: lots of money. If our capital markets provide any insight to human behavior and motivation, then we have an extraordinary peek at opportunism and the Western World's insatiable appetite for wealth accumulation.[5] During the 1990s, greed was running on overdrive. Even though the level of IPO and acquisition activity is down during the period 2000–2003, we should remember that it is almost exclusively a function of poor market conditions. The conditions may have changed but the organizational systems that will allow this behavior to occur have not changed. Consequently, it is quite possible that in the absence of organization or regulatory reform, some of this behavior will someday return.

Going Public—The Ultimate Harvest Vehicle?

It shouldn't be surprising that the greatest excitement in an emerging growth organization often centers on the prospect of an IPO market. From the outset, many entrepreneurs and financiers

---

5. Arguably, not since Holland's 17th Century tulip craze have markets witnessed such a feeding frenzy and out-of-control escalation.

see the IPO as the ultimate harvest vehicle. Why? Newly listed companies have an established fair market value that sets an immediate, and many believe unbiased, estimate of the firm's true value. An IPO facilitates team building and incentive alignment as well as prestige and stability of capital structure. It also provides liquidity. Whenever an equity holder wants to cash out, he just calls a broker and gets his money transferred into his brokerage account in seconds. This doesn't happen with privately held ownership. Holders of private stock may never be able to see their stock, and even if they do sell, will probably pay high transaction costs and get a lower price than they wanted.

The mere prospect of "going public" is daunting. Of the millions of newly created ventures each year, only a handful ever makes it to the public offering stage. Financial statements need to be cleaned up, the story or "road show" needs to be prepared, and everybody involved with the deal needs to be onboard. Everybody sings the same tune, and outside investors receive a constant message. Basically, outside investors want to hear about how a unique team, with extraordinary talent and vision, will take their investment dollars and build a new empire to ever greater heights. Sometimes it works (Home Depot) and sometimes it doesn't (eToys). Sometimes it works for a while and then later doesn't (Boston Chicken). However, the basic approach doesn't change—investors want growth and will quickly bid up a company's stock if they see evidence that the story is working. Investors will also punish the stock if they discover that the story is a lie.

There are plenty of participants outside the company that help bring the company to market and facilitate the development of the story. These include corporate accountants, lawyers, investment bankers, and venture capitalists. Some of these participants get fees as a percentage of the deal size (investment bankers and financiers) some receive stock with ownership (venture capitalists). Some earn more fee income as the deal increases in size and complexity (accountants) and a few earn fee income along with stock in lieu of fees (some lawyers earned "founders stock"). Thus, as much as corporate managers want to receive a higher price upon sale, there is an equal or greater amount of pressure pushing the price higher on the outside of the company.

Those participants who support the stock price realize how fickle the markets can become once the truth emerges. Because inside owners (such as venture capitalists) are usually required to vest or hang onto their holdings for 6 to 12 months after an IPO (restricted or limited stock sales), these folks have to watch in horror with everyone else if the stock price falls precipitously shortly after going public. Although there is potentially a lot of money to be made for a successful IPO venture, there is considerable effort and risk with this approach. That is yet another reason why most deals didn't harvest or cash out through an IPO. The vast majority of harvests occurred through a strategic sale, acquisition, or consolidation (combination with another company in a similar area). This was the primary method during the 1990s and it allowed key advisors, stakeholders, and sellers to get their cash out immediately. It was particularly attractive for those dealmakers that wanted to liquidate their holdings and transfer their funds to safer or more diversified havens before the bad news leaked out.

Ways to Grow— Complex Problems... So Little Time

The short-term orientation among stakeholders is not a trivial issue. This track did not start yesterday and it will not disappear tomorrow. If anything, given the changing corporate landscape, this myopic approach is likely to get worse. Years ago, employees came to a firm and had a long-term orientation. The company was their future and individuals were very protective of their workplace and organizational assets. Nowadays, corporate employees, particularly senior executives, are likely to last only three to four years. This short-term duration changes everything. Corporate loyalty has become a thing of the past. Sure, some people still follow the corporate mantra and sacrifice for the benefit of the organization. However, this attitude becomes less likely when the people hiring inform the people interviewing that they themselves do not expect to be at the firm longer than a few more years. Should you be surprised that some executives and employees game the system for personal benefit? Moreover, if this is the approach among members *within* the organization, should we be surprised if members external to the company have the same attitude as well? Collectively, this *can* be a rather big problem for a large organization. Actually, it would be more accurate to state that it *is* a major problem for large companies. There are many terms used to define this issue, but the most commonly applied descriptor is "corporate culture." Corporate culture, it seems, is the all-encompassing, universal "umbrella" adjective that quickly encapsulates all that is good or bad about a specific organization and its people. But what is it really, and can it be harnessed for useful purposes? Some of it comes from the people currently working at the firm but much of it may simply come with age and accumulated bureaucracy.

Why Acquire? Why Not?—It's Fast

Executives of large organizations realize that the lifeblood of corporate health depends on new business initiatives and growth.

But what is the best path of growth? Organic growth is not easy and it may be that management pursues acquired growth simply because it is the best way to shake up the organization and move it forward. Organizational size and age influence corporate culture and the active pursuit of opportunity. As a general rule, older companies tend to have lower levels of organic or internal growth and more mature product lines. Also, these older and larger companies tend to be less entrepreneurial. Consequently, in the absence of corporate reinvigoration or opportunity pursuit, decay will set in and corporate atrophy will occur. Perhaps this is why many *Fortune* 500 CEOs pursue acquired growth in such an aggressive manner. Acquired growth, although not as desirable as organic growth, may be perceived as more desirable than the alternative of no growth. Plus, acquired growth is fast. Companies can double organizational revenues or assets in a matter of a few weeks. This might take 10 or more years through internal means. For many large, older companies, they might not otherwise ever get to these milestones. Acquired growth may be the only sure growth they've got.

Why Acquired Growth Doesn't Work— Who Stays and Who Goes?

When companies acquire other companies, they usually consolidate operations and attempt to implement synergistic cost-savings and efficiencies. In simple terms, this means some redundant jobs will be eliminated and people will be fired. This leads to a vicious, self-indulging circle of events on Wall Street. Because firings improve financial statements, executives plied heavily with stock options can use this mechanism to boost stock prices and indulge Wall

Street. Consequently, people get fired—lots of people. Large company mergers engender interest and popular press attention because the big companies have large layoffs. Who stays and who goes hinges on logistics, efficiency, and corporate politics.

Not surprisingly, employee morale suffers from M&A transitions, which often bring internal retaliation and sabotage in various forms, such as theft of intellectual property, malicious destruction, and spirited arguments. Calm and order within the organization may take a long time to return. Some firms never recover. Internal mistrust and perceptions of greed and exploitation offset the perceptions of improved efficiency. Continuing collaboration among parties may be strained to the point of dysfunction. At the extreme, parties unite along territorial boundaries based on the original alliance, with each sharing a common hate for the other side. Teamwork deteriorates and organizational integration fails to materialize. In essence, all that appeared positive on paper disappears in a muddle of political sniping and infighting. Growth suffers.

For many acquisitions, the simple consolidation and elimination of jobs is much easier for the accountants and the deal analysts than for the front-line managers. The anxiety and heartache for paring inefficient operations is real, and maybe even inevitable. Accomplishing the cost reduction through consolidation and subsequent divestiture generates unnecessary transaction fees benefiting only the dealmakers. Many deals look good on paper and, in actuality, should be completed. The evolution of business forces efficiency and refines the business model. Needless expenses or redundant costs *should* disappear. However, the manner in which cost efficiencies develop does not mandate industrial consolidation or a transfer of ownership. Indeed, a simple cross-border alliance might be all that is required.

Inevitably, some cross-border deals will occur and ownership rights will transfer from one party to the other. Leaders will emerge to drive the new organizations to higher levels. But ownership transfers need to consider the cultural differences among the different groups and the damage done from an inappropriate consolidation. Some value-added members of the team may transfer or leave during the shuffle, thus compromising the future direction of each new unit. Adding two units together and then splitting them apart comes at a cost. Prior to bringing together two different organizations, business leaders need to be able to anticipate whether the organizational conflicts representing different cultures will more than offset the benefits related to the consolidation. Future growth depends on this important assessment.

Changing Goals and Culture Over Time: We Need a New Model of Growth

Young companies, particularly young companies in the process of going public through an IPO, generate strong excitement. All members within and outside the firm seem focused on this wealth-creating event. Management can easily rally support and push energized team members to perform beyond expectations. Personal and professional goals may never again be so perfectly aligned with a large group. An IPO provides focus and congruence to organizational goals while creating an economic harvest for its stakeholders. Even those employees who do not own a direct stake in the company's stock get excited about a potential trickle-down effect of wealth. It is clear throughout the organization that a significant, dynamic situation will occur and that all stakeholders can benefit from success with this event. Moreover, just subsequent to the IPO, interest is piqued. The company is in the spotlight, executives appear flawless and productive, and well-groomed employees smile for the cameras. Things in Corporate America just don't get much better than this. With the new equity infusion, management becomes blessed with new problems: how to best allocate the newfound infusion of cash.

As long as the stock continues to rise, management can feel proud of their contributions and can point to the market's reaction as support for their actions. But over time, the company and stock may encounter dips. Along with increased volatility of the stock price, employees and management may begin to develop diverging views regarding their organizational and personal goals. Entering employees may come in with fresh energy and a naïve perspective about rising through corporate ranks to the top. Middle managers may become jaundiced by unfulfilled dreams and resentment for institutional hierarchy. Senior managers might focus on stock movements without regard to equitable allocations among other members of the organization.

Each group may expect different things from the organization and be willing to contribute different things to it. With these changing dynamics and departure from goal congruence may come the answer as to why the for-profit organization cannot sustain itself over long periods of time.[6] Perhaps the key differential between for-profit ventures and nonprofit institutions has more to do with goal congruence among the stakeholders and less with organizational efficiency and change. Maybe large companies cannot survive long term because the institutions are filled with myopic members, each of whom seeks a different self-motivated path. Perhaps the different paths that drive members of a firm are a

---

6. Unlike some non-profit organizations such as churches, colleges and political institutions last hundreds or even thousands of years.

function of people coming into the organization from different upbringings or orientation of life. Maybe the only time when company employees really get along and agree on the organizational goals are when they first set up a company or are about to take one public. Suppose these are the reasons for institutional lethargy. What needs to change?

Organizations need to create new ventures with a new model of growth that can operate within the limiting facets of the general environment and corporate culture. True growth will depend on strong leadership to craft new solutions that motivate current and future stakeholders. Much of the outcome may be generated with appropriate incentives and clever personnel. These may come from organizational design and structure. Changing the company culture and environmental orientation is a different story. This will be near impossible to accomplish. Great leaders will either learn how to embrace and manage the culture or learn how to effectively get around it.

Is Acquired Growth Any Good— Let's Look at the Evidence

During the height of the M&A craze, we initiated a study of growth-oriented firms. We discovered that acquired growth firms performed worse than the industry benchmarks (i.e., average firms). These data are consistent with other studies examining acquired growth. However, our tests explored a different wrinkle compared to other tests. Our investigation showed that organic growth companies provided superior stock results. Further, the study confirmed that many of the highest paid executives were using acquired rather than organic growth as the method of choice to grow their organizations.

Is Acquired Growth Any Good—
Let's Look at the Evidence

In testing this hypothesis, we compiled a list of 50 highest growth companies from the *Fortune* 500 annual listing and ranked these companies based on growth in revenues and assets for a five-year time period (1995–2000). Each company was then examined for growth through either acquired or organic means. This meant that we had to evaluate each acquisition for amount and relative impact to the firm and examine annual reports (e.g., income statements, balance sheets, and statement of cash flows) for other financial information and transactions. We used a number of databases popular with academics (e.g., SDC, CRSP, COMPUSTAT, Moodys, etc.) to help us with our research of company acquisitions and employed an arbitrary cutoff in determining organic or acquired growth.

In evaluating our data we were really interested in just one key question: Do organic companies provide better stock returns to shareholders than acquired growth firms? The results follow.

Growth in Revenues Does Not Equal Growth in Stock Price

The vast majority of our high-revenue growth companies (44 of the top 50) grew principally from acquisitions with many of the companies being well-recognized names such as Enron, Cisco, MCI WorldCom, 3Com, and Lucent. *However, we were curious to know whether high-revenue growth necessarily translated into greater shareholder return.* Our data did not provide this support. In fact, during the five-year period, the top firms in the acquired growth cohort earned considerably less for their investors (535%) compared to the return earned by organic growth companies (3832%).

Is Acquired Growth Any Good—
Let's Look at the Evidence

2001 to 2003—Post-Evaluation Period

When we compared the performance during the recessionary period 2001–2003, we found that high-performing organic growth companies were more likely to rebound more quickly than acquired growth companies. We found that acquired growth firms averaged a *negative* 68% return compared to the *positive* 15% return earned by organic growth organizations during these two years. These results may be noteworthy for several reasons. First, not only did the acquired growth cohort significantly underperform the matched grouping of organic growth firms (e.g., –68% vs. +15%), but the acquired growth firms significantly underperformed all of the major market indices as well (e.g., –68% vs. –19% for DJIA).

Ironically, during 1999 several companies that had experienced great success with organic growth abandoned the traditional model and began either aggressively acquiring other companies (Qualcomm, Sun, or EMC) or merged with another large organization (AOL/Time Warner). In each of the cases in which management switched growth strategies, poor stock returns followed (this group earned –77% on average during the subsequent two-year time period).

Conclusions

The data provides some evidence that organic growth organizations provide greater shareholder returns than acquired growth organizations and perhaps more important, than the overall benchmark portfolio. This occurred during both bull and bear markets. Furthermore, many of our strong

Is Acquired Growth Any Good—
Let's Look at the Evidence

revenue-growing companies had executives who either were listed among *Business Week*'s top paid executives, were involved in management impropriety, or both. Because acquired growth can accomplish an organizational overhaul very quickly, it is probably not surprising that this methodology has been subject to abuse. Ultimately, our evidence shows that the shareholders lost, despite earlier indications that the organization might perform well.

Although acquired growth does not benefit shareholder wealth creation, it may offer a path for senior management to create personal wealth. Given their relatively short stay at the top, they may have had incentive to promote M&A activity to foster growth, facilitate a culture change, or manipulate a stock option harvest. Furthermore, given the large wealth transfer that accompanies M&A activity, we hypothesize that many deals may also have been attributed to other "Agency Costs" associated by harvest incentives of investment bankers, venture capitalists, and other financial advisors.

Organic growth firms did not experience these same consequences. The evidence shows that (1) growth in revenues did not necessarily lead to growth in stock price and (2) the best growth (from a shareholder perspective) came from organic or internal means. Organic growth companies provided investors with the best long-term benefits.

Is Acquired Growth Any Good— Let's Look at the Evidence

The data suggest that the markets ultimately reward growth created the "old fashioned" way—through clever market expansion, internal cost-cutting, strategic direction, and other methodologies used to expand through traditional internal means. Organizations that did not develop long-term value through internal means ultimately experienced a severe market correction. Given the run-up in some valuations through the mid- to late-1990s, the market correction for some organizations was well into billions and for some, hundreds of billions of dollars. Cisco, Nortel, Lucent, Daimler/Chrysler, and AOL/Time Warner are just a few of the companies that experienced billions of dollars of lost market value.

6

A NEW GROWTH
MODEL

Bureaucratic Companies Begin
as Entrepreneurial Firms

Long before large, public organizations become stagnate and
sluggish, they often begin as small, entrepreneurial companies. They
have dynamic, visionary leaders driving their organization forward
through innovation, charisma, and hard work. As these companies
grow and expand their market share, individuals flock to them
seeking employment. And why not? They're on a roll. They have
momentum. These high-growth companies have the opportunity to
select the best and the brightest. They raise cheap capital from the

U.S. capital markets through an IPO and *everything* seems to be going right. They have bright, happy people, plenty of cheap capital to fuel expansion, Wall Street analysts singing their praises, and soaring dreams and stock market capitalization. Nothing can slow them down. Yet, predictably, perhaps inescapably, large organizations ultimately experience both a product and an industry life cycle decline.[1]

Why can't large organizations continue to grow for long, uninterrupted periods with energy, excitement, and dynamic, contributing employees? Part of the answer is that products may become mature and obsolete over time. Perhaps it also hinges on a corporate culture that rewards certain behaviors detrimental to long-term growth. Stakeholders who maximize their own self-interests may tug the large company in lots of different directions. Ultimately, these companies can splinter apart after a period of wealth transfer and decay. *Fortune* 500 companies have a lot of experience in this area. Typically, the large company receives no economic benefit. The revenues go to the newly formed company. In some cases, a parent organization loses out on an entirely new industry.

If Only They Had Stayed...

Over the years, Bell Labs had 11 Nobel Laureate winners among its staff, yet many of them chose not to stay. Some left to pursue academic careers whereas others formed a new venture. In one notable example, Dr. William Shockley departed Bell Labs after 19

---

1. See, for example, *Fumbling the Future*, Smith and Alexander, William Morrow, 1998. In this book the author describes how Xerox missed out on a number of key opportunities.

years of service (he joined after earning his Ph.D. from MIT). He went to California to start up a company named Shockley Semiconductors and later became a Stanford Professor. Dr. Shockley earned a Nobel Prize in 1956 for his work in developing transistors at Bell Labs, but it was his contributions in helping develop "Silicon Valley" for which he may have arguably achieved greater fame. After working for one to two years developing transistor technology, a number of Dr. Shockley's hand-picked assistants (also known as "The Traitorous Eight") left him to join a growing firm known as Fairchild Semi Conductors.[2] This group included a number of technological pioneers (e.g., Robert Noyce and Gordon Moore, founders of Intel) who later left Fairchild and created their own firms. In total, Dr. Shockley was the catalyst for bringing in people who were directly responsible for the formation of 30 Silicon Valley ventures! These firms included some of the largest in Silicon Valley, including: Intel, National Semiconductor, Advanced Micro Devices, Teledyne, Rheem, LSI Logic Corp, Kleiner, Perkins, Caulfield, and Byers.[3] In retrospect, Bells Labs may have missed out on a great opportunity but who knows if this movement could have ever been created in their corporate environment? Besides, Bell Labs is not alone in this arena. Great companies attract great people and sometimes an established "star" employee departs, taking away great organizational

---

2. As an interesting aside, the founder of Fairchild Semi Conductors, Sherman Mills Fairchild, was the son of George Fairchild, the founder of Computing, Tabulating and Recording Company (CTR). CTR later became International Business Machines (IBM) with Mr. Fairchild serving as the first Chairman. Much of the success of IBM is credited to Thomas Watson who was hired away from National Cash Register (NCR), where he was a senior executive (from Fairchild and IBM Company Reports).

3. "Fairchild's Offspring," *Business Week*, August, 25, 1997. See also, "The Startup Culture," Silicon Valley.Com, February 28, 2002.

potential. Sometimes the entrepreneur is a virtual "unknown" who develops an idea (on the side) while working full time. And, sometimes a charismatic CEO brings in a talented entrepreneur only to read about how the individual left his firm and created his own successful venture a few years later.

There are plenty of examples in which a company missed out on extraordinary revenue potential. But does it have to turn out this way? Getting a little piece of something has got to be better than the alternative. What follows is a small sampling of: "What could have been."

- Bell Labs: Nobel Laureate leaves the company and initiates a chain of events leading to the development of "Silicon Valley" (Intel, National Semiconductor, AMD, Teledyne, etc.).

- National Cash Register (NCR): This company lost a senior Vice President named Thomas Watson. He left to join a start-up that developed into a multibillion dollar enterprise named IBM.

- Digital Equipment: Robert Ryan was a rising star at Digital Equipment, before leaving to create a few new firms on his own. He later sold his best known venture, Ascend Communications, to Lucent Technologies for $23 billion in 1999.[4]

- Motorola: After a 29-year stint at Motorola, Martin Cooper, known as the inventor of the first portable, wireless phone, left his position as Director of R&D and founded several new companies (one of which was later sold to Cincinnati Bell).[5]

- General Magic: Pierre Omidyar was a software engineer when he first created a company for the purpose of selling Pez containers on the Internet. His online auction house later turned

---

4. See, for example, "Ascend Communications Founder is CU Entrepreneur of the Year," *Cornell Chronicle,* May 16, 2002.

5. Mr. Cooper is now Chairman, CEO, and founder of ArrayComm (Array-Comm.com annual reports).

into a company better known as eBay and in 1999 was worth $11 billion. Considering that the parent, General Magic, was worth only $160 million, it shows how sometimes even middle managers have ideas that can contribute.[6]

- Apple Computers: Sabeer Bhatia decided to join Apple Computers after listening to an inspirational speech (at Stanford University) from Apple Computer CEO Steven Jobs. Bhatia stayed at Apple for a few years, and then jumped to a software developer for a couple of years where he came upon the idea of a web-based email service. He later sold his company, Hotmail, to Microsoft for an estimated $400 million.[7]

- Battelle: In 1944, the Battelle Memorial Institute contracted with patent lawyer and part-time inventor Chester Carlson to refine a new process called "electrophotograpy." This new process was designed to replace carbon paper. A few years later, Battelle provided the rights associated with Xerography (Greek words for dry and writing) to The Haloid Company. Haloid later coined the name "Xerox" and established an enormous market presence in the photocopying industry. Since its inception, Battelle has had other similar experiences. For example, it created the technology for the UPC scanning labels and compact discs (among other notable inventions).

- Xerox: The wealth transfer for Xerox has been well documented. The book *Fumbling the Future* describes how this innovative company has either directly or indirectly been responsible for the creation of the personal computer, computer mouse, laser printer, and many other companies, products, and technologies (e.g., Adobe Systems, etc.).[8]

---

6. See Garage Technology Ventures, "Investor Nugget of the Week," Rich Karlgaard, Forbes Publisher, February 24, 1999.

7. "Hot Idea Delivered Instant Wealth," Tom Anderson, *Oakland Tribune,* April 29, 2002.

8. Fumbling the Future, Smith and Alexander, William Morrow, 1998. See also, "Battelle Innovations," Battelle.org or Xerox at emediaplan.com.

Corporate America Needs to Capture the Growth of New Ventures

Large, public organizations need a facility that captures the growth that may be incubating within their walls and that may soon depart. Managers need a model that rewards risk-taking and provides incentives to those who develop intellectual capital. They also need a model that steps aside from the corporate bureaucracy and enables them to negotiate with entrepreneurs inside the company or that may approach them from outside. The growth template should leverage the intellectual property, distribution networks, and cheap/easy access to capital made available by the parent organization. It should also facilitate strategic expansion, new product development, new market entry, and cultural change to the parent organization. Furthermore, the approach should encourage the same cost-oriented, value creating, entrepreneurial mindset and spirit of a small company. But, the growth model should not be encumbered by the parent's sluggish culture or management's greed. Otherwise, costs may escalate with no one paying the price but the residual shareholders. Finally, the growth model needs to be insulated from self-serving venture capitalists, dealmakers, research analysts, and other consultants or advisors that might drive management into behavior that serves special short-term interests. But does such a model incorporating all of these factors exist? If not, what approaches have been tried in the past that come close to handling these criteria?

From Spinouts to Corporate Venturing: Growth Models Past, Present, and Future

Many of the factors described earlier have been incorporated into new venture growth models. Indeed, managers of large companies have recognized that corporate opportunities have been lost in the past, and are constantly experimenting with new approaches in an attempt to capture new venture growth. A very brief summary of some of the applicable models in this area follows. These include: (1) a model of Corporate Intrapreneurship (attempting to grow a new business within the big firm, (2) an approach to Corporate Spinouts (a mechanism for the parent company to harvest a new venture that it believes no longer has strategic value and that can operate more efficiently on an independent basis), (3) Corporate Venturing (an approach to take the VC model inside the large company), (4) Corporate Venturing with a Venture Capitalist (this is the same as the Corporate Venturing Model, but in this situation the Venture Capitalist adds funds to the parent firm's contribution and offers its network an independent perspective), and (5) SEU Model (this approach offers a blend of the other models and offers the entrepreneurs an equity stake and operation control while leveraging the parent firm's intellectual property and financing on an arm's length basis).

Corporate Intrapreneurship

The Corporate Intrapreneurship model (see Figure 6.1), first introduced in the 1970s, attempts to create new ventures within the organization. The parent organization selects "entrepreneurial employees" and selects an area that it perceives to have high growth potential. It creates a new company that may be resident in the same physical space as the parent company or moved to another location. The parent organization controls the operations, owns all of the equity, and performs all of the deal and employee selection. Further, the parent company provides all of the funding and determines the Board of Directors/Advisors. Because the new ventures are completely contained within the Parent organization, the new ventures are subject to the funding and political whims of executives within the parent.

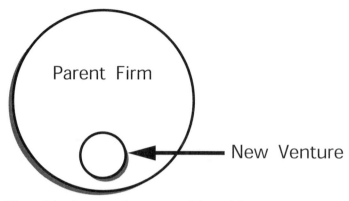

Figure 6.1   Corporate Intrapreneurship model

Corporate Spinouts

Corporate spinouts (see Figure 6.2) are generally considered a way in which the parent company sells its stake in a wholly owned venture. In some cases the parent sells all of its equity ownership and in other cases the parent sells a partial share. Generally, the parent sells when it believes it no longer has a strategic interest in the new venture and when it believes the venture may be more valuable with an independent relationship. During the mid-1980s through the 1990s, companies such as Thermo Electron experimented with an "extreme version" of this model by assisting 12 of its ventures to raise funds through an IPO. In the case with Thermo Electron, the parent company maintains a strategic link to each venture and allows operations to run independently with direct equity incentives for entrepreneurs and senior stakeholders in each venture.[9] The Spinout approach allows entrepreneurial employees to remain focused on activities that are being closely monitored by public shareholders and other stakeholders. Perhaps owing to the equity distribution, spinouts generate high corporate loyalty among venture employees.

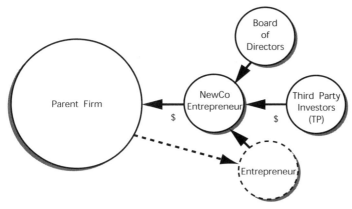

Figure 6.2   Corporate spinout model

Corporate Venturing

During the mid- to late-1990s, large companies started using the VC method for high potential ventures. This approach within the big company, known as "corporate venturing," has been popular among companies such as Nortel Networks, Cisco, Lucent, Xerox, and so forth that allow internal managers to apply a VC-type of approach in evaluating high potential investments. Large companies set up separate business units with

---

9. For example, over the 12-year period 1984–1995, Thermo Electron increased revenues 20 times (from $200 million to $4 billion) through its spinout model, which provided key employees an equity stake in a venture. Of the 23 new ventures created, they had an 85% success rate and 12 IPOs were created. See *New Forms of Organizations*, The Wharton School, University of Pennsylvania, March 18–19, 1999. Also, see *Venture Catalyst*, Donald L. Laurie, Perseus Publishing, 2001. Yet only a few years later, after a loss in one of the spinout divisions led to a decline in the parent's stock price, the strategy was reversed and the spinout divisions were either re-absorbed or divested completely. According to some analyst reports, the spinouts were seen not to have had enough control over their own destiny and required administrative support functions that could have been shared with others within a conglomerate; see Vecta on Spinouts," Vecta Consulting Limited, 2002.

their corporate venturing managers taking a high-risk/high-return perspective in sorting deals, selecting employees/entrepreneurs, financing, and harvesting. In the early years of corporate venturing, deal flow had a "strategic orientation" with the parent company. During later years, there appeared to be a move toward financial return (based on our survey of corporate venturing executives). Also, very few companies (Nortel Networks being one of the exceptions) provided an equity stake in the new venture to existing employees/entrepreneurs. The Corporate Venturing approach was very popular, but executives reported numerous problems associated with internal politics, company culture, and deal selection. Both compensation and corporate culture were cited as major impediments to maximizing growth. Figure 6.3 shows an example of how a corporate venturing model was set up.

Corporate Venturing with Venture Capitalist Participation

Sometimes corporate venturing executives invite venture capitalists into their deals (e.g., if a Lucent or Cisco Ventures group was to invite Battery Ventures or Kleiner Perkins into a deal). Bringing a VC firm into a deal not only expands and diversifies the capital base (i.e., more funds could then be allocated against more deals), it also expands the network of entrepreneurs/employees and strategic partners. Furthermore, and perhaps more important, it provides an independent perspective on the deal and the participants involved. As an independent party whose primary interest may be to maximize financial return, the venture capitalist acts as a catalyst in assembling the right team and partners to maximize the potential of the new venture. With

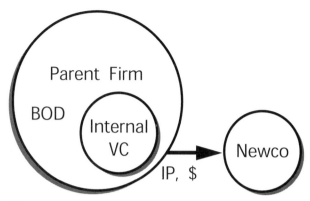

Figure 6.3   Corporate Venturing

their investment into a fund (or specific deal), venture capitalists assume a position on the Board of Directors and can help steer the new venture in a manner that benefits their stakeholder interests. However, because venture capitalists require a financial return, they tend to focus on generating a harvest (strategic sale, IPO, etc.). This may not necessarily be in the long-term interests of the parent organization or the members within the new venture. An alternative approach (see Figure 6.4) using SEU attempts to mitigate these concerns.

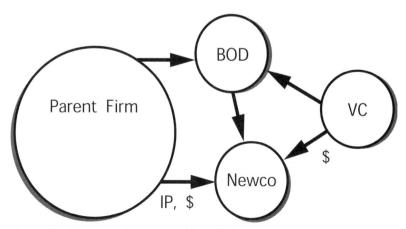

Figure 6.4   Corporate Venturing with capitalist participation

SEU

The SEU approach is a modification to prior corporate spinout and venturing models and suggests changes in the manner in which companies handle deal selection/filtering, third-party financing, negotiations with entrepreneurs/employees, applications of intellectual property, and harvests. This new approach does not apply to every organization and every situation. Companies that have invested energies and resources in existing growth templates will probably not want to change. Many other companies do not have the appropriate culture to implement innovation. However, this approach may offer potential for some large companies attempting to extend their growth cycle. The SEU model is really just a combination of a few old models with a new twist.

SEUs: A Combination of Old Models with a New Twist

The SEU model incorporates compensation incentives for value-creating entrepreneurial employees and, similar to the spinout model, attempts to keep highly motivated individuals within the corporate organization umbrella. Further, just like the spinout model, the SEU approach does not eliminate problems related to corporate culture, but avoids them by moving the growing organization to a separate operating unit altogether. It essentially attempts to replicate the situation of an entrepreneur leaving an organization, with the twist that the parent firm remains involved (to the extent that it adds value).

The SEU takes part of the corporate venturing model approach in that it attempts to apply the parent company's strategic orientation, intellectual property, and capital. It also introduces the non-corporate perspective of the venture capitalist by bringing in experienced, independent outsiders (Facilitators) to help manage the deal selection, negotiations, and financing relationships. However, the SEU approach is different from the VC model as it does *not* allow the Facilitator to determine the timing or type of harvest. The SEU allows all parties to work in their own best interests, while also creating value for the parent firm. However, it is not a riskless situation.

Employees who seek entrepreneurial rewards will be required to take some level of entrepreneurial risk. But, similar to the logic of the corporate venturing model, given the brand, infrastructure, and access to resources, the risk to the entrepreneurs should be lower with the SEU and the returns should be higher than if the individuals were working completely independent of the parent organization.

Organizations that set up SEU ventures should consider investing with a "portfolio" perspective. This is the manner in which venture capitalists and professional money managers handle their investments. For example, SEUs could be diversified by a number of factors including: year of investment, size, number of deals, location, stage of investment, and so forth so that the total performance of the SEU portfolio is not dependent on a single project (i.e., don't put all eggs in one basket). This means that although any individual SEU may prove unprofitable, an organization with a whole portfolio of projects is spreading its risk around so that in the end the overall mix should prove to be very valuable.

The SEU facility explores wealth creation through collaboration and sharing. It provides entrepreneurial employees an opportunity to live out an entrepreneurial dream without taking the risk of setting up an entirely new venture and to partner with the parent firm. Consequently, these employees, or entrepreneurial partners, are called "EntrePartneurs." This is very similar to the logic in a corporate spinout approach but does not go to the same extreme (where the spinout is completely funded by external equity capital in an IPO). However, this presumes that people within the organization are entrepreneurial in mindset and ideology. In practice, a self-selection bias may exist wherein individuals attracted to entrepreneurial ventures may not reside in or be attracted to a large company. Thus, a more likely model may incorporate individuals from outside the company who have the capacity and willingness to assume the higher risk-return trade-off. This latter approach is referred as a *Reverse SEU*. In practice, most companies are not readily set up to handle this inquiry. The closest example might be an entrepreneur approaching a VC and asking for funding along with a corporate partner.

Reverse SEU—The Start of Xerox

The history of Xerox suggests that it, in fact, was an example of a Reverse SEU situation. In 1944, when patent attorney (and part-time entrepreneur) Chester Carlson finally persuaded Battelle Memorial Institute to assist him with his electrophotography process, it was *six* years after he created his patent. Mr. Carlson later commented that business executives and entrepreneurs didn't think that there was a market for a copier when carbon paper worked appropriately. Further, Mr. Carlson's prototype for the copier was unwieldy and messy, making it even less attractive as an alternative. In total, approximately, 20 companies, including IBM and General Electric, met with Carlson in what he referred to as "an enthusiastic lack of interest."[10] Clearly, the effort and value of Mr. Carlson's vision paid off, but we can only imagine the number of ventures that have not been realized over the years due to resistance from corporate staff and insufficient perseverance from the entrepreneur. The Reverse SEU approach facilitates growth with entrepreneurs coming to the large company from outside. The SEU structure simplifies the terms of the deal and more easily accommodates the sensitive negotiations and disputes on a timely basis. The details of the SEU are discussed later.

Anatomy of an SEU: Getting Between 0 and 100%

The basic structure of an SEU begins with the deal and its strategic orientation to share some of the value created with the parent, entrepreneurial employee (or entrepreneur outside the firm), and other key stakeholders. Without a strategic fit, the deal might still be feasible, but it falls under the umbrella of financial investment and does not pertain to this model template. The demarcation of an SEU mandates that the deal relies on intellectual property, distribution mechanisms, or personnel within the parent organization but resides outside the traditional arena of normal research and development. The SEU template also applies to traditional blocks within the parent organization but in those areas that fail to deliver the compensation incentive necessary for new intellectual property formation. The structure of the SEU enables the parent and entrepreneur to navigate the treacherous waters between 0 and 100% ownership and control.

---

10. See the Xerox Web site for its corporate history, or Xerox at emediaplan.com, 2002.

Figure 6.5 shows the formation of an SEU. Basically, there are only a few key components to the SEU diagram: (1) large organization (contains the intellectual property, capital, infrastructure, and human capital), (2) Facilitator (unbiased mediator that handles key negotiations among participants—discussed in greater detail later), (3) SEU (high-potential venture otherwise known as "the Deal"), (4) Board of Advisors (members within and outside the organization), (5) third-party financiers (risk capital providers that are not related to the parent organization), and (6) EntrePartneurs (entrepreneurial employees or entrepreneurs outside the firm who are seeking equity in a venture and a partnership with the parent). There may also be potential alli-

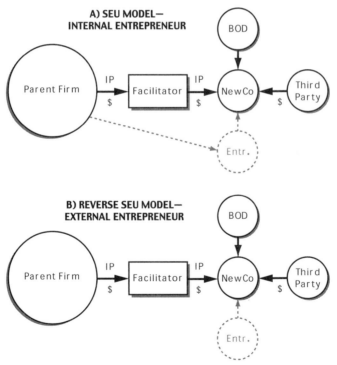

Figure 6.5 The SEU model

ance partners but these will be brought to the Facilitator to decide how to handle.

The SEU model has many of the same key factors as the Spinout and Corporate Venturing models. However, there are some important differences between this model and the others. For example, the compensation is not set up with a simple static (i.e., constant) weight or percentage, but rather varies from deal to deal. Moreover, the financing is not limited to the parent or a specific dedicated fund, but again has the flexibility to vary. The board of advisors has a blend of participants, but the financier (if outside funds are solicited) cannot drive the firm into a harvest. Finally, the SEU Model introduces a new participant, known as the "Facilitator," that provides many of the functions of an independent venture capitalist (unbiased perspective, catalyst to deal development, arbiter to conflict) but without the focus on harvest. The Facilitator is a key member of the SEU concept, which is discussed later, along with the other value drivers in the deal formation (e.g., compensation, intellectual property, board of advisors, financing, and harvest).

Facilitator—A VC without the Equity, Control, and Harvest Motivation Role of the Facilitator

Each party to the new venture may differ in outlook and strategic view of the harvest. The potentially disparate goals represented by different stakeholders complicate the situation for the venture management and owners to satisfy. The SEU model proposes using an independent third-party Facilitator to help address and negotiate these conflicting pressures between the EntrePartneur, large corporation, and outside investors.

This means that the Facilitator should make the EntrePartneurs feel comfortable sharing intellectual property with them. EntrePartneurs need to be able to trust that the Facilitator is an independent, unbiased party who will protect their ideas and help determine whether the idea is worthy of continued pursuit. The Facilitator negotiates the terms of the deal (between the various parties) and sorts out the ownership rights associated with current and future intellectual property. Because any new venture frequently has many changing dynamics including funding, development of intellectual property, strategic alliances, personnel mobility, liquidity, and strategic alliances, the third-party Facilitator also fills the role as overseer of conflict resolution. This Facilitator is very different from traditional venturing models in that the Facilitator, and not the VC, helps decide important compensation, intellectual property, financing, and conflict issues. The Facilitator receives both fee income and a small equity stake, but cannot force liquidity through an IPO or strategic sale. By design the Facilitator will *never* be allowed to have enough power to exert control in this manner. This is an important distinction from the VC model and it removes a potentially destructive conflict of interest.

More strategic, contentious problems handled by the Facilitator include, but are not limited to: timing of harvest, market valuation, new directions, growth, investment, equity distribution, ownership and licensing rights of intellectual property, new partners/affiliates, and personnel. If the Facilitator is handling his responsibilities properly (and frequently the Facilitator will be a group of qualified professionals), very few of these contentious issues should come as a surprise. The Facilitator should be able to anticipate the potential for conflict and be prepared to handle the problem without serious disruption to the enterprise or extensive litigation. Remedies for immediate resolution may include binding arbitration and, for more serious disputes, provisions to dissolve their continuing relationship. The Facilitator, again, needs to focus on maximizing the value of the deal and keeping all eyes focused on this agenda. The Facilitator holds the responsibility of keeping lines of communication open and reducing potentially damaging exchanges between the parent and entrepreneurs and treating both with respect and confidentiality.

Compensation—Providing More than a Salary

The compensation element in the SEU model is another key component that drives value creation. Without providing individuals an economic incentive to keep the high potential venture within the parent firm, entrepreneurial people will have motivation to leave and take their intellectual property with them. This means that entrepreneurs who provide the firm with exceptional opportunities should be able to generate exceptional equity-like returns. On the other hand, managers and entrepreneurs who bring in standard skills and work ethics commensurate with industry norms should receive no more than average compensation. This means that average performance does not earn equity. This concept should be clear throughout the parent organization and SEU. To receive above-average compensation, the parties must bring exceptional skills, intellectual property, or financing to the deal.

Equity Grants

For purposes of efficiency in distribution, actual equity shares will be shared with relatively few participants. However, equity-like compensation should be available to any number of members affiliated with the deal. Those individuals not receiving an actual equity stake should have compensation incentives based on net revenue milestones or clear contribution margins. Members eligible for equity participation should include, but not be limited to: key EntrePartneurs, strategic partners, executives from the parent who officially moved to the SEU, financial partners, the Facilitator, Board of Directors, and other strategic participants.

Normally, when entrepreneurs internal to the organization approach the parent with an idea, they quickly realize the distorted balance of power. The parent has the infrastructure and financial capability to completely run the negotiations. This enables the parent to take full advantage of the situation. Consequently, it is a rare event in which an employee is provided an equity stake.[11] The imbalance of power may actually motivate entrepreneurs within the firm to withhold information from the parent and take their venture outside the organization.[12] Furthermore, because individuals tend to be averse to risk, it is likely that the only members who would be willing to leave a relatively safe corporate environment

---

11. In our survey of corporate venturing executives, Nortel was one of the few firms providing equity to employees.

12. Theoretically, it is possible that entrepreneurs might prefer to let the deal die (rather than share with members of the organization) but it may be more logical that members of the firm (who don't leave) simply keep this information in the event they are terminated. This information could be used as a negotiating ploy to gain entry in a new job, or as a back-up plan to initiate a new venture.

with salary and benefits would be those individuals who have great confidence in their new venture. Ironically, this implies that if organizations refuse to share any equity in new ventures, they may unintentionally force out the best and most promising entrepreneurs and their high-potential possibilities.

What If It Doesn't Work?—Lifeline Back to Parent

One of the more controversial issues regarding compensation relates to the lifeline back to the parent. On the one hand, if a lifeline is extended back to the parent, the individual departing the parent is not really acting as an entrepreneur. A "true" entrepreneur makes his or her own decisions without a safety net or guaranteed income stream. Most of the great entrepreneurs of the 19th and 20th century journeyed into unknown business terrain without any downside protection in the event of failure. That's an important part of the risk/return trade-off. On the other hand, most of the employees working for a publicly traded, *Fortune* 500 firm are probably not entrepreneurs—otherwise they would likely be working at a different, albeit, smaller, private organization. It is this self-selection bias (e.g., large firms are not likely to attract "true" entrepreneurs) that makes the lifeline such a controversial dilemma.

The SEU template demands that individuals seek exceptional risk/return paths. Large, publicly traded organizations need to shake up the conservative middle management that may have lost incentive to grow the organization or work efficiently. Somehow this group in the middle of the parent company needs to see opportunity that can radically change their lives for the better. Whether or not they are willing to embrace opportunity may be a secondary, albeit important, consideration, but they must see that there will be no free lunch. If individuals within the organization want exceptional compensation, they will need to deliver exceptional performance and incur additional economic risk.

Harvest:
The Key Driver in Most Deals

No single event or situation galvanizes institutional energy or excitement like a potential harvest. On the one hand, the harvest can provide focus to all shareholders. Each party works hard to ensure financial success. All eyes are glued to specified targets and all energies are harnessed to meet ever higher milestones. This part of the equation is a beautiful sight. On the other hand, the appearance of large sums of money changes the attitude of some people who may focus on self-serving payouts and "retention bonuses" rather than creating future value for the shareholders. Consequently, the harvest may present both a blessing and a curse to its stakeholders.

Those in power often position themselves for this once-in-a-lifetime situation. The traditional VC model has incentive clauses that force or encourage a harvest, even though it may create unnecessary transaction costs and undermine the long-term value creation process for the shareholders. The SEU approach eliminates the requirement for a strategic sale or IPO, thus minimizing the transaction costs associated with a harvest.[13]

The SEU model addresses both the ability to motivate and create value among worthy entrepreneurs and the opportunity for participants to liquidate or harvest their wealth without overly taxing the enterprise with excessive transaction costs.[14] It allows a simple conversion of the SEU's private stock into the parent's publicly traded stock at a clear price.

Intellectual Property: Who Owns What?

Organizations need to be very careful about releasing strategic data. The intellectual property issues are often litigious problems that need to be carefully evaluated in the context of ownership rights among the parent, entrepreneur(s), and SEU. The clear demarcation of ownership and continuing value creation should be determined at the start of the venture. However, because much of the intellectual property may fall into potentially gray areas, it is best for all parties to have clearly defined borders, a priori. This will reduce needless litigation and allow all parties to focus on value creation.

A big advantage of the SEU template is that it forces stakeholders to discuss intellectual ownership and rights before the venture begins selling product and/or services. By establishing the

---

13. As we discuss later, because large publicly held companies already have marketable, actively traded stocks, the SEU template saves at least 7 to 10% on transaction fees. Shareholders in the SEU can trade their ownership with the parent's publicly traded stock and avoid the need to sell the venture that would otherwise be necessary to "cash out" members of the deal.

14. Dealmakers often refer to actions and costs associated with dissolving an entity as "unwind provisions."

ownership rights and responsibilities, it helps clarify what each party brings to the negotiating table and how each of the parties can leverage their respective talents and resources to build value going forward.

Financing: Expanding the Project Beyond the R&D Budget

Considering that the parent has a strategic advantage in accessing cheap capital, there can be few alternatives better than using the parent as a source of cash. Few organizations in the world have access to the amount or rate of a large, publicly traded, *Fortune* 500 organization. Long-term public debt, bank borrowings at rates below the prime rate, large lines of credit, publicly traded stock, shelf registrations, collateralized receivables, and commercial paper are all some of the forms of cash available to a large, public organization. Indeed, the interesting dilemma of large, publicly traded organizations is that they tend to experience slow to negative growth *despite* their access to cheap capital. SEUs need to utilize this strategic resource in an appropriate manner and be careful not to use too much capital simply because it may be readily available. At the same time, the parent needs to protect its organizational ratings and not get carried away with large investments in risky ventures.

This is one of the advantages of the SEU. It enables the growing venture to diversify its funding and not be entirely dependent on the parent organization for future financing. All risk capital, including the funds contributed by the parent, should enter the SEU in an arm's length contract (i.e., fair market price). This means that any new venture should expect the capital to be priced at VC rates (or whatever is deemed appropriate for the amount and risk level). Any expenditure or service provided by the parent should also be treated as a contribution to the SEU and priced accordingly. For example, if the SEU borrows office space from the parent organization, the SEU should be charged a fee at market rates. If the SEU requires input from the parent's corporate lawyer, then the parent's attorney should be charged to the SEU at the market rate. In other words, all products and services should be priced to the SEU at fair market value. In the event the SEU is unable to pay with cash, the parent may consider a swap to provide services or loan cash to the SEU in lieu of additional equity in the new SEU venture.

All financings should initiate with, but not be restricted to, the parent. For example, the SEU structure might benefit with cash infusions from other stakeholders including the entrepreneur, management team, and affiliates. Further, if the cash infusion from SEU stakeholders and parent is insufficient to grow the business, the third-party Fiduciary has an obligation to seek venture financing from external parties including traditional venture capitalists, but should attempt to bring in risk capital from passive investors who will not try to manage the deal.[15] Although the politics of the SEU template have been designed to reduce external influences that have traditionally been detrimental to long-term value creation, the design still allows external cash flows to easily enter the system.

---

15. Passive investors tend to be investors that are only seeking a return on capital and are not trying to be "active" in their management of the transaction.

Board of Advisors:
Who Drives the Direction?

External advisors to the SEU should include financiers, representatives from the parent, entrepreneurs based in the SEU, a third-party Facilitator, other strategic advisors, and possibly an elected shareholder from the parent organization. The external advisors have the sole purpose of maximizing the value of the deal and should attempt to increase the growth of the SEU through whatever channels best help meet this need. It would be helpful if the advisors had at least some minimal equity stake in the SEU venture and this could be arranged through either direct sale or distribution in lieu of cash compensation for Board services rendered. Because some members of the Board might potentially have an economic stake in the new venture, measures should be taken to prevent a potential conflict of interest.

Summary and Rationale of SEU

Many major, public companies in corporate America might benefit from a heavy injection of entrepreneurial behavior. There is, of course, nothing urgent pressuring these companies to do so. In some respects this is unfortunate. At least with a major calamity or crisis, management can rally around a purpose and central mission statement and work together to solve the problem. Slow, organizational death is a more insidious and difficult problem. Sometimes the remedies create more trouble than the problem itself.

To grow successfully, organizations should try to emulate the competitive entrepreneurial edge similar to what they had in earlier stages of corporate life. By allowing small groups to operate as independent, albeit affiliated members, the parent can become more profitable and be able to grow its core business faster. This is important. The parent can grow bigger by pushing growth to smaller, affiliated units. These smaller units can then better manage their human resources and focus on their narrow component of the value-added chain. In the aggregate, the high growth from many small units could well exceed the small growth from the balance of the firm. Furthermore, the parent can better integrate all of the pieces for economic gain and utilize its market position to acquire less expensive capital. This will help improve the margins for the small units in the future.

The best way to maintain or create momentum for the large firm is by creating a facility that enables some entrepreneurial employees an opportunity to create equity in their own ventures. This approach may even be more successful for bringing in entrepreneurs to the big firm who are currently outside. Providing equity returns or partial ownership in a small venture helps focus the attention of entrepreneurial employees. It provides a path that enables individuals more control of their future and greater influence in the development of their career. This approach is already well established in our marketplace and used by small, entrepreneurial firms. The difference is that small entrepreneurial companies now compete against large companies; they're not part of them.

Large firms may be able to grow efficiently by investing in a portfolio of small growing firms that are managed as entrepreneurial ventures. In the end, if the small firms grow bigger, the large firm will grow bigger as well. This is the thesis of the SEU concept: Big firms get bigger by growing through smaller independent units.

Summary

Table 6.1 provides a summary of traditional models of venturing. Table 6.2 provides a summary of the SEU model.

Table 6.1   Traditional Models of Venturing

	Corporate Management	Entrepreneur	Facilitator
Compensation	Management determines the compensation for entrepreneurs and itself. A potential problem exists if entrepreneurs or venture capitalists earn more than senior management. Also, a potential problem could develop if the entrepreneurs perceive that senior management earns too much relative to their contribution.	Management decides the amount of compensation earned by the entrepreneur. A potential problem exists if the entrepreneur does not engage in equity-type compensation or believes that the company will not provide adequate compensation relative to contribution.	A potential problem exists if senior management or the entrepreneur(s) believe the venture capitalists are gaming the situation to their advantage. If venture capitalists do not see an adequate return they will avoid opportunity.
Control	Traditionally, large companies are reluctant to give up control. Consequently, many entrepreneurs may choose to avoid any new initiative (out of concern that company politics/culture will destroy the opportunity) or leave the organization where they can exert more control.	Entrepreneurs traditionally have very little input into the decision or development. They tend to be completely dependent on the parent for financial and institutional support. Moreover, given the intellectual property (IP) issues, they may not have the flexibility to lease or rent the IP or decide on the appropriate path of development.	Venture capitalists may initially begin with relatively little control or influence, but may increase their control as the deal approaches a harvest opportunity. At the point of harvest, given the venture capitalist often becomes the driving force and actively solicits investment bankers and deal partners to initiate a bid (i.e., purchase) or IPO. In the absence of a potential harvest, the venture capitalist may look to bring in a new team or move the IP to a group that can increase the likelihood of a potential harvest.
Conflict resolution	Parent is generally not inclined to negotiate as an equal partner. The parent usually owns or controls the IP and controls the financial contribution; the parent is therefore reluctant to casually relax this strategic advantage when negotiating with an employee or third party.	Employee/entrepreneur usually has relatively weak position vis-à-vis the parent, and is usually reluctant to disclose all plans. The employee may ultimately leave the organization with controversial levels of IP or fail to pursue new initiative (for fear that others will profit at his expense). Entrepreneur usually has no third-party representative except for litigious conflict.	Venture capitalists often provide some external perspective for corporate managers and entrepreneurs. Given the contractual nature of their work, venture capitalists usually side with the corporate parent on most critical issues.

Table 6.1　Traditional Models of Venturing　(Continued)

	Corporate Management	Entrepreneur	Facilitator
Intellectual property	Management usually assumes that all intellectual property is owned by the corporation and will often engage in significant legal battles to protect such property. Any new IP created by a separate venture needs to be negotiated prior to development.	The entrepreneur often has a different view on the ownership and potential utilization of IP created by himself or the group. This divergent view may result in potential conflict with management and be subject to unpleasant negotiations with the corporation. Moreover, to the extent that the entrepreneur knows that his views are far apart from management's view, he may decide to leave the organization with controversial IP or decide not to pursue the new venture.	Venture capitalists do not usually develop the IP, per se, but may be instrumental in the continued nurturing of such work.
Impact to others not directly involved with deal	Generally management does not address those who are not directly related to the new venture.	The entrepreneurs do not address those who are not part of the key team.	Venture capitalists do not focus on any parties not directly involved with the venture.
Risk aversion	Management offers a "one size fits all" plan for entrepreneurs. Given the large number of employees, it is usually very difficult to provide individual plans for each employee, unless the employee has exceptional or unique talent.	Entrepreneurs usually have a self-selection bias in the pursuit of a new venture. Those entrepreneurs attracted to unique risk/return characteristics will probably never pursue a career path at a large organization. Those who develop an entrepreneurial flair may do so with limited risk exposure.	Venture capitalists usually have greater upside potential, given their investment and intellectual property contribution, and need to justify their value-added through deal flow and harvest realization. They usually demonstrate the most entrepreneurial behavior of the participants at the negotiating table, as they are able to command an equity stake without a direct contribution to the initial IP generation.
Final goal—development and organizational structure	Incorporate new venture into organization. Instill entrepreneurial flair into organization and jump-start growth overall. Increase organic growth along with financial return. Reduce likelihood of stagnation.	Increase financial gain and improve career path. Increase control and direction on career pursuit and initiate entrepreneurial adventure. Straddle safety net with parent while exploring independent venture.	Maximize financial gain and improve industry network and skill expertise. Develop interlocking resource base increasing likelihood of future deal flow and harvest opportunities.

Table 6.2   SEU Model of Corporate Venturing

	Corporate Management	EntrePartneur	Facilitator
Compensation	Management earns an amount commensurate with perceived value-added contributions. Moreover, management will prepare a board to oversee, represent, and negotiate the organization's interest in the new venture. Management may or may not earn more than the entrepreneur, but both entrepreneur and management earn more than the external third party.	The entrepreneur has an opportunity to earn an equity stake and contribute to the cash investment into the new venture. Moreover, the equity stake may be calibrated depending on the risk aversion of the entrepreneur(s) and the level of incremental investment and contribution of the various parties. Because many entrepreneurs may be risk averse, some members of the same team may have a different base salary and equity stake component.	The third-party Facilitator will generally earn a combination flat rate plus success fee. However, the fee structure cannot be open-ended (i.e., without ceiling), nor can the success fee exceed the contributions of either management or the entrepreneurs. Both the entrepreneurs and management should share any direct fee payments to ensure that a client bias does not enter future deliberations.
Control	Companies will have control over any IP rights deemed owned by them, but will not necessarily have control over the future development or direction of the new entity. Any funding of the new venture or use of administrative support will be entered into at an arm's length basis. The company will have a put-and-call option available to exercise for the harvest and should have a right of first refusal on any future investment.	Entrepreneurs traditionally have very little input into the decision or development. They tend to be completely dependent on the parent for financial and institutional support. Moreover, given the IP issues, they may not have the flexibility to lease or rent the IP or decide on the appropriate path of development.	The third-party Facilitator will earn a fee along with a small percentage of the equity but will not be able to exert control on this deal. Unlike either the corporate parent or entrepreneur, the third-party Facilitator does not have a put-or-call option in the deal. The third party has no control on the terms of the deal, but has considerable flexibility on the evolution and development of the deal. Unlike a VC, the third party is not focused on a harvest of the deal, but rather, earns a fair fee for services rendered as the deal progresses.

Table 6.2 SEU Model of Corporate Venturing (Continued)

	Corporate Management	EntrePartneur	Facilitator
Conflict resolution	The third-party Facilitator negotiates the terms of the deal and decides the appropriate percentages for both parent and entrepreneur. As part of a concession to the SEU arrangement, the parent realizes that negotiations will become more balanced than in the traditional situation. However, the parent must be convinced that in the absence of a third-party participant, some deals may not materialize or some deals may not develop to full potential.	The entrepreneur can bring "proprietary" deals and information to the third-party Facilitator with confidence that a fair analysis and negotiation will be forthcoming. Consequently, more deals should ultimately surface and fewer deals should leave the organization.	This is the principal purpose of the third-party Facilitator. The sole purpose of this group is to protect the interests of the deal. The Facilitator should act as a mediator to maximize the value of the deal and consider all parties' interest to meet this primary purpose.
Intellectual property	The third-party Facilitator will negotiate the terms of the IP and handle any issues related to the sharing of any IP owned or controlled by the parent or entrepreneur.	The third-party Facilitator will negotiate the terms of the IP and handle any issues related to the sharing of any IP owned or controlled by the parent or entrepreneur.	The third-party Facilitator will negotiate the terms of the IP and handle any issues related to the sharing of any IP owned or controlled by the parent or entrepreneur.
Impact to others not directly involved with deal	Management and the entrepreneur will receive the largest equity stakes, but some equity returns may also be earned by the third-party Facilitator and external financiers (e.g., venture capitalists). Furthermore, other managers not directly involved in the organization may receive compensation for supporting roles (advisors, consultants, etc.). The purpose of this compensation is to ensure that a zero-sum game is not perceived by those not directly involved in the transaction. This may also facilitate the team concept employed within the organization and encourage general support and nurturing for new ideas rather than resentment.	The entrepreneurs may receive the largest equity stake for the new venture (measured on an individual basis), but may not be confined to only these employees. Management, including senior management and other support managers, may also receive compensation or a sharing of the prize, upon harvest, to encourage organizational support and nurturing.	The external Facilitator should identify other internal and external parties that may potentially assist with the development and growth of the new venture.

Table 6.2   SEU Model of Corporate Venturing (Continued)

	Corporate Management	EntrePartneur	Facilitator
Risk aversion	Management can offer a flexible salary/benefit plan by utilizing an external party to determine the appropriate compensation arrangement.	Entrepreneurs usually have a self-selection bias in the pursuit of a new venture. Those entrepreneurs attracted to unique risk/ return characteristics will be eager to pursue equity return and may want to exercise an option to increase an equity stake through additional invest-ment or salary/benefit reduction. Those who are interested in nonfinancial gain may request a less variable risk/return trade-off and work with the Facilitator to accomplish this objective.	The Facilitator needs to address the unique needs of the entrepreneur(s) and help calibrate the equity/ salary stake in the new venture. This is a critical role of the Facilitator in the development of the new initiative.
Final goal	Management would like to incorporate the new venture into the organization and instill entrepreneurial flair into the organization. The hope is that this will jumpstart growth overall, increase organic growth, and improve the financial return. This should reduce the likelihood of stagnation.	Increase financial gain and improve career path. Increase control and direction on career pursuit and initiate entrepreneurial adventure. Straddle safety net with parent while exploring independent venture.	Maximize financial gain and improve industry network and skill expertise. Develop interlocking resource base, increasing likelihood of future deal flow and harvest opportunities.

7

IMPLEMENTING THE SEU

The path to corporate growth through small ventures begins as soon as the organizational leader or CEO decides to implement an SEU. This provides the necessary impetus to commence growth plans. Compensation parameters need to be established, along with an SEU template. Internal and external notifications need to be sent out along with a clear methodology for idea generation, filtering, and potential funding. Most important of all, the Facilitator, SEU board of directors/advisors, intellectual property rights, and equity distributions need to be made clear along with operational independence from the parent. If the SEU is to have any legitimate chance of entrepreneurial growth and value creation, it needs to have an organizational structure and management team that emulates entrepreneurial conditions. Presumably, key management has already recognized the institutional advantages of an SEU format and the need for the new ventures to be separated from large corporate culture and politics. Otherwise, the establishment of an SEU and costs associated with implementation may become a wasteful exercise.

When to Use an SEU

The reasons to use an SEU are not unlike the reasons for using any new venture model. Managers may consider a new start-up venture for reasons beyond the obvious urge to break in on the ground floor financially. Financial investment growth has been a primary driver in the past decade and continues to be one today. Throughout the 1970s, 1980s, and 1990s, many firms invested in ventures of all types, including close, strategically orientated projects (e.g., extensions of existing in-house projects, such as Campbell's adding a new line of soups) and those that are more distant from operations, but pursued for purely financial results, like Phillip Morris investing in a software firm that promises a quick revenue turnaround. In the latter case, the proximity to the core business did not seem to matter so long as a financial return was attached. In fact, one corporate venturing executive cited the move away from strategic to financial goals with the comment, "There is nothing strategic about losing money." This particular statement summarizes the move toward financial return at precisely the time when organizations were flush with cash and there were an abundance of attractive investment options outside of the firm. Many corporate venturing initiatives turned their attention away from "strategic growth" within their own organization and started to focus their energies on "financial growth" away from their firm (i.e., independent projects that may or may not have had any strategic link to the core business operations). However, the economic collapse from 2000 to 2003 put corporate venturing into a new perspective. Many of the corporate venturing funds collapsed and many of the project investments were completely written off. There were few, if any, added benefits or synergies to the investing company, as the pursuit was purely financially motivated. However, projects that have a "strategic orientation" with the company may provide additional rewards. These include at least four primary reasons to formulate and start an SEU in addition to pure financial gain. These reasons are often interrelated:

- Strategic expansion of the firm into new areas
- Technological acquisition
- New product development/market entry
- Implementation of cultural change
- Strategic expansion

Management in a large firm may believe that growth in its core business, although vital, is less attractive than growth in other businesses. This creates a dilemma for operating managers that need to decide between focusing on the strategic fit of new growth initiatives and creating short-term financial gains in areas that may not be germane to everyday activities. By funding initiatives that are outside the firm's core activities in an SEU venture, the company can monitor these more remote businesses without severely taxing or burdening its manpower, organization, or customer areas. If the new SEU venture is constructed properly, it will create unique new value for the firm along with long-term financial gains.

Technological Acquisition

SEU ventures, not unlike other corporate venturing initiatives, should grow faster than in-house development projects because they contain motivated entrepreneurs expending energy and independent focus on their own ideas, free of corporate bureaucracy. Pursuing a new SEU venture may also be less expensive than acquiring an established company that may bring with it undesirable side effects (e.g., different culture, work ethic, etc.) that undermine the entire organization. SEU ventures may provide a hedge against in-house development without diverting or detracting management from their daily activities. Finally, the SEU venture can also incubate innovative technologies without fear of diluting the core focus of the parent organization.

New Product/Market Access

An SEU can be the means to access either new products or new markets without placing a burden on the existing structure of the firm. Expansion into new markets often requires local knowledge or expertise. The new SEU can provide that knowledge without requiring the larger firm to step in and utilize its own resources (financial, management, people). A product or market that is completely removed from the existing operations of a firm can be allowed to develop at its own pace without straining the resources of the parent corporation.

Cultural Change

A start-up SEU may be utilized to foster or experiment with an organizational concept, compensation technique, or employee relations approach that is too radical or unproven to risk being implemented quickly in an established firm. Structured and bureaucratic organizations are slow to embrace new concepts and often resist any overt attempt to change. Using the SEU as a learning laboratory or experimental site permits the concept to be tested, tried, and evaluated for full incorporation into the core company at a subsequent time period. Examples include geographic location of key expertise, cross-functional teams on projects, or equity grants based on performance in the venture. The cultural change may also take on a newer role in terms of "re-energizing" the companies' employees. With spirit, vigor, and high energy being likely characteristics of new ventures, these types of people/energies may influence the parent organization and help facilitate greater motivation and increase in productivity.

Creating new SEUs external to the large organization makes sense for a variety of reasons. But given the reluctance of internal management to address change, how does the organization implement a new SEU within the walls of the parent? For many companies, getting a new initiative started becomes a major challenge and institutional constraint.

Steps in Implementing the SEU

The steps of implementation require the organizational leader to take a step back and allow the role of the Facilitator to perform his or her fiduciary obligations and do what is in the best interest of the SEU venture. But, for even this to occur, two primary catalysts must occur: the selection of the Facilitator and the selection of the business idea.

Selection of the Facilitator

For the Facilitator to be effective in his or her role within both the large organization and the SEU, it is almost imperative that the Facilitator be independent from the large organization. But why is this so? In one study, approximately 86% of employees do not feel comfortable approaching their managers or senior leaders with business ideas. They mention lack of "trust" and "comfort" as the two primary reasons.[1]

For an SEU venture to take place with an affiliation to a large organization, it is vital that the Facilitator build trust with the employees of the large company so that they feel comfortable discussing their ideas and intellectual property. Furthermore, the employees must believe that if they come up with the idea the Facilitator will ensure that they are properly compensated in the new venture. Otherwise the SEU venture may have difficulty attracting internal participants.

One of the most important decisions in embarking on an SEU is the choice of the Facilitator. Many organizational managers will not easily agree to let a third party resolve intellectual property rights or make decisions about external compensation issues. These responsibilities of the Facilitator may coincide with or even replace

---

1. Research conducted at Babson College, 2003 (assisted by S. Taub). A total of 400 surveys were sent out to *Fortune* 100+ companies (both public and private companies). Survey respondents included: 274 fully completed (68.5%), 50 partial, and 76 nonreturns. These employees were entry level as well as lower and middle management.

those of key senior managers. This is likely the most contentious issue in the SEU template. However, it is also at its core. Without an SEU Facilitator to moderate or mitigate conflicts or to handle sensitive negotiations, the large company ends up with an internal model that is doomed to all of the problems described earlier. Large companies require a different model that encourages and facilitates entrepreneurial talent to bubble up from within, or approach from outside. Existing growth models do not easily accomplish this task.

What Type of Company Could be a Facilitator?

There are a number of companies (and/or individuals depending on the size of the company) that can easily fill the role of the Facilitator. Interestingly enough, many of the companies that previously provided risk financing to large companies can also provide these services, but they are not the primary focal point. Risk capital providers tend to have a harvest orientation toward the small ventures and may not have long-term shareholder growth in mind. However, there are four basic criteria that the Facilitator needs to meet. These include:

- Must be independent

- Must be separate legal entity

- Must conduct or have access to technical evaluation of SEU idea

- Must have access to capital (either an angel network or other third-party investors to bring to the SEU)

A prospective Facilitator may not meet all these criteria per-fectly. For example, the fourth criteria states that the Facilitator must have access to angel investors or third-party capital. Although it is ideal that the Facilitator be able to secure funds outside of those obtained from the large organization, it is not necessary (or even desirable) that the Facilitator provide the funds directly. Simply having an appropriate network to bring to the negotiating table should be sufficient for meeting the responsibilities in this requirement.

Furthermore, although the Facilitator role may best be handled in a long-term manner with relatively little turnover, it should be clear to the Facilitator that it is not a job with entitlements or permanence. If intermediate to long-term targets are not met, the Facilitator could (and should) be replaced with other talent.

Given that the SEU is a relatively new concept, it will not be possible to find a consulting individual or company that features services directly targeted for SEU formations (though over time this will change). However, the types of companies that can provide these Facilitator services include the following:

- Consulting companies that are moving into business services

- Accounting firms moving into services

- Large business service firms

- Spinoffs from large company development activities

- Investment bankers who are expanding into services

- Turnaround specialists

- Former entrepreneurs

- Retired business executives

As a starting point, the large organization needs to prepare the initial due diligence, customize the general SEU template, and meet with a variety of potential Facilitator candidates. The large company should then prepare a "short-list" of potential candidates (i.e., those that met their threshold to conduct business) for the SEU entrepreneurs to select from. Consequently, both the large organization and the SEU entrepreneurs have input in the selection process and should feel comfortable sharing sensitive information with the Facilitator. The notion of a Facilitator "short-list" keeps each of the Facilitators at arm's length and encourages competition among the different prospective participants, even after a selection has been made (i.e., in the event the large company or SEU wants to later change). Given the requirements of expertise, there are likely dozens of different companies, and literally thousands of individuals, that would be able to meet the demands of the SEU Facilitator role.[2]

Responsibilities and Duties of the Facilitator

The Facilitator will fill two primary job functions within the large organization: (1) provide a filter of business ideas from within and outside the organization and (2) third-party arbitrator of the negotiations within and between the SEU and large organization.

In the first role, the Facilitator will differentiate or "filter" good ideas from bad. Further, the Facilitator should become a familiar, trustworthy figure to whom employees can discuss various ideas

---

2. Note: Although the Facilitator would ideally encompass a firm (with varying expertise, etc.) it is possible that an individual (e.g., retired business executive or accomplished entrepreneur) would be able to handle the duties of Facilitator for small venturing activities. However, the very nature of the SEU venture requires expertise in many different areas including: negotiations, technical knowledge, network, and so forth that may best come from an existing organization with diverse talent.

they might like to explore. Employees throughout all departments and ranks should feel comfortable forwarding their business plans or ideas to the Facilitator who will then select among those that merit additional attention.

Once an idea has been selected by the Facilitator, it is then polished to present to those individuals inside and outside the firm for potential funding. At this time (coinciding with the SEU formation), the Facilitator helps negotiate the terms of the intellectual property rights and distribution (if any doubt exists), leasing, ownership, or rental terms of intellectual property, allocations of equity interests among deal participants, and the handling of conflict resolution as problems arise.

Because the Facilitator may be assisting multiple employees/projects during the same time period, there may be a need to help navigate various projects and ideas at different stages of development. Consequently, the Facilitator at a major firm needs to have a full team facilitating the deal process, disseminating information, and negotiating a variety of deals at the same time.

After the legal paperwork formalizing the SEU is complete (much of the paperwork should be standardized), the company can pursue financing and assembling its key team of entrepreneurs/employees. As an unbiased third party, the Facilitator should assist with much of this process.

The Facilitator in the SEU

After successfully gaining approval among key decision makers to establish the SEU, the Facilitator becomes an essential catalyst in growth formation. The Facilitator becomes involved almost daily with various roles and functions within the SEU and provides numerous functions in addition to deal flow generation and filtering. They include but are not limited to the following:

- Clearinghouse for deals
- Business plan catalyst
- Lead negotiator
- Equity distributor
- Compensation developer
- Management consultant
- Conflict arbiter
- Noncore service provider
- Compensation of the Facilitator

Some of the services occurring at the early stages of SEU development (e.g., deal filter and business plan facilitation) provide a direct benefit to the large organization and should be paid for corporate cash flows. Once the SEU is established and funded, it should pay for any continuing services or obligations. This means that the Facilitator is being compensated directly by both the large company and the SEU. Consequently, the Facilitator is not entirely independent (as mandated in the template) as there is the potential for bias depending on the amount, timing, and expected delivery of future cash flows. However, where possible the SEU template should impose a process that minimizes the threat of bias by the Facilitator.

The Facilitator should be excluded from the Harvest decision and have no economic bias surrounding a final sale or IPO. Also, the Facilitator should probably not be a voting member of the Board of Directors, although the Facilitator's presence at Board meetings may be allowed (or even encouraged). Further, where possible the SEU should build in various success or bonus payments to the Facilitator for specified targets or goals. The primary source of revenue to the Facilitator should derive from ongoing services to the SEU (i.e., outsourcing for payroll, accounting, staffing, etc.). In this manner, the Facilitator will derive economic incentive to build the SEU into a larger, more secure company. As the SEU increases in size it will command more services that will directly benefit the Facilitator.

The Facilitator should be granted some large deferred bonus payments, in lieu of cash payment, in the early stages of the business plan development. Otherwise, the Facilitator will be creating a role not unlike a classic venture capitalist with a harvest incentive. The Facilitator should not be placed in a position where there is an economic incentive to force the company toward an early or convenient harvest. The primary role of the Facilitator should be in developing the value of the SEU and this goal should not be comprised or motivated by an opportunistic harvest.

SEU Equity and Distribution

One of the toughest decisions in the beginning will be in allocating the equity among all of the key stakeholders. The Facilitator will be central to the decisions in helping determine the appropriate distributions. The SEU equity should be allocated among seven basic constituencies: (1) the large (parent) organization, (2) the EntrePartneurs or entrepreneur(s) outside of the organization ("Reverse SEU"), (3) third-party financiers, (4) the Facilitator, (5) the new venture board members, (6) the entrepreneurial employees or EntrePartneurs within the SEU, and (7) a safety bucket (for other key stakeholders and unforeseen circumstances).

Although the precise level of equity participation will vary with each organization depending on intellectual property rights, entrepreneur contributions, and third-party financings, the relative equity contributions should be reflected in ownership allocation per Table 7.1.

The possible range of equity participation reflects the terms that might be entered into under the SEU indenture or legal document. However, as a practical matter, it may be preferable to set a desired target or "ideal" range for equity participation as shown in Table 7.1. Although it may be easiest to allow the parent the largest and majority ownership (i.e., equity) stake, it may not be in the parent's long-term interest to do so. Thus, it may require some ingenuity to draft an agreement (through IP leasing rights or short-term rights of application) that allows the SEU entrepreneurs to participate in a significant manner. In the absence of a worthwhile ownership stake for the SEU entrepreneurs, it may be difficult to garner the entrepreneurial spirit necessary to grow the venture. Further, if the equity stakes are not balanced according to some predetermined ranges, problems may develop later that might potentially undermine the long-run growth of the SEU venture or strategic link to the parent.

Table 7-1   Equity Allocation

	Range of Equity	"Ideal Target Ranges"	Recommendation
Large Organizations	10-90%	20-49%	40%
EntrePartneurs	10-80%	20-60%	25%
Facilitator	0-10%	1-5%	1%
New Venture Board Members	0-10%	1-5%	3%
Other Employees	0-20%	0-10%	1%
Third Party Financiers	0-50%	10-30%	20%
Safety Bucket	5-15%	5-10%	10%
Total			100%

Table 7.1 shows a preferred range for the parent organization in the 20 to 49% level with 40% being the desired target. This provides the parent organization significant ownership rights but does not provide for operational control. Because the SEU should evolve as a traditional entrepreneurial unit, keeping the parent's ownership less than 50% will be helpful to ensuring relatively low interference in day-to-day operations.

The preferred equity range for EntrePartneurs is in the 20 to 60% area with 25% being the desired target. Although the entrepreneur partners may be entitled to a small equity percentage for having put together the deal, it is their continuing efforts and sacrifice of secure salary and benefits that earns them a higher stake. The entrepreneur stake should be sufficient to motivate this group, but not be so high as to alienate or generate animosity among the other key stakeholder groups.

The Facilitator, for all of the duties and functions he or she performs, will receive no more than 5% of the SEU's equity, but most likely fall to approximately 1% of the stake. The Facilitator will spend considerable time working with the entrepreneur(s) from start to finish, but his or her compensation, as stated earlier, should primarily derive from fee income and bonus.

The New Venture Board members should receive more than a relatively small stake in the venture and should not have a significant ownership. The range for this group should fall in the 1 to 5% ideal range with 3% being a reasonable target.

Third-party financiers, other employees (key stakeholders), and a cushion or "safety bucket" (to be distributed as needed) should comprise the remaining shares. This additional equity may amount to 30%+ of the organization and should be allocated as the needs require.

New Venture Board

The composition of the SEU board should reflect the ownership stakes and interests of the key stakeholders. Certainly among the members are the lead entrepreneurs with voting privileges, along with a representative from the parent company. The parent can select a member from its new business ventures group (if one exists) or may select a member from its strategy group. The Facilitator should also be a member on this board, however in this model will not have voting privileges when it comes to the final exit strategy (unless the Facilitator has an insignificant ownership stake). The Facilitator should be allowed to vote on other items. Without some voting power, the Facilitator cannot truly maximize the SEU venture and have a voice in steering it toward its potential. If there are any third-party financiers, they should have a representative on the board as well. However, any third-party financiers should realize that the SEU is not set up with a time clock or harvest strategy.

Implementation Summary

Large, public organizations need a new approach to growth. They need a model that rewards risk-taking and provides incentives to those who develop the intellectual capital as well as those members that seek an entrepreneurial path. The new growth template should leverage the intellectual capital, distribution networks, and cheap access to capital made available by the parent organization yet not be encumbered by the parent's sluggish culture or management's greed. Further, the new model needs to be insulated from self-serving venture capitalists, dealmakers, corporate officers, and other consultants or advisors that might drive management into behavior that serves special short-term interests at the expense of long-term wealth creation.

The SEU template is not perfect and does not fit all organizations. However, it offers better flexibility and ways to achieve long-term growth for the large organization than other models that typically reward short-term financial gains. The model attempts to minimize the potential for economic bias and behavior among stakeholders that could undermine the long-term development of the SEU. However, so long as any economic model is dependent on paid consultants (such as a Facilitator) for advice, it is always possible that personal motivation will bias the results. But this should not imply that a system should be banned for its imperfections. Rather, it offers a starting point for further refinement and application.

The SEU model uses an unbiased third-party Facilitator to act as an intermediary between the parent and entrepreneur. The parent may argue that this Facilitator introduces yet another layer of oversight, cost, and delay that could be handled within the parent organization. This will likely be untrue. Although management may not welcome a Facilitator entering the SEU template as a participant that usurps its duties and responsibilities, the relatively small deals suited to the SEU template would otherwise be too time-consuming for senior management to oversee.

Existing venture models need some modifications to make them work better! Entrepreneurs within a company often do not share their insights or expertise. Large companies are thus losing entrepreneurial opportunities each year, along with the potential for added revenues and profit. Things need to change for the large company if they are to grow stronger over time. The SEU model, with the proper oversight from senior management (at the parent company) and implementation of an independent Facilitator, provides a workable solution.

8

FINANCING AN SEU VENTURE

Equation for Growth:
Moving Big Company Risk Capital to SEU

Big companies have money. Lots of money. In fact, large, publicly traded organizations have the cheapest capital of any company on the planet—by far. Inexpensive capital may be their single most significant comparative advantage over small companies. It's a shame that they frequently squander it on items that don't help them grow stronger.

Fortune 500 companies have public stock, public debt, collateralized debt, debt with enhanced credit ratings, supplier financing, and in a few situations, commercial paper (short-term debt issued

141

directly to the investor). This means large companies, in addition to all of their advantages with manufacturing economies of scale, intellectual property, R&D, and specialized management, can put the power of cheap capital to work so as to beat all others. They have the ability to approach the investor directly and can raise *billions* of dollars in a couple of hours simply by posting an interest rate on a Telerate, Reuters, or Bloomberg terminal. Some companies, such as Ford Credit or GE Credit, do this every day.

Financial giants can bypass the financial intermediaries altogether and save on high transaction fees by placing their money directly with the investor. Major companies have more funding sources, lower interest rates, lower transaction fees, and immediate access compared to small companies. Yet, despite these enormous advantages, large companies frequently fail. It seems that being successful at raising cheap capital is not the same as being successful. Obviously there is more to the equation than just getting money. Large companies need to have good investment opportunities and an efficient structure to manage their investors' capital. This is where the SEU ventures come in.

Taking the risk capital from large companies and placing it into a few select small companies provides a great equation for future growth. Small companies need to be more careful or more efficient with spending, due to their difficulty in raising risk capital and its cost. Moreover, because small firms tend to be managed by watchful owners/entrepreneurs, there might be less waste of company assets. This suggests that the potential of bringing together the cheap capital from large companies coupled with the efficiencies incorporated in small companies provides the makings of a great combination.

This is the basic premise of the SEU approach: take cheap, easily accessible risk capital from the big company and put it to work in a portfolio of small, high-growth (and efficient) small companies. Entrepreneurs and key stakeholders in the SEU should have equity and an opportunity to gain liquidity in their holdings, but should also have protections against a premature harvest. Finally, the risk capital should be managed like any other professional venture fund. This means that the fund should be diversified into a variety of different investments and funds should be allocated during both strong and weak economic conditions.

Combine Low-Cost Funds with High-Return Ventures

Risk capital should be invested as long as the return exceeds the cost of funds. This concept is basic to fundamental business practice and to sophisticated compensation mechanisms.[1] However, small companies, due to their brief track record and lack of profits, often have relatively high default risk and few, expensive financing options. Large companies, on the other hand, have relatively low default risk and many, inexpensive financing options. So why do large companies with their many advantages and low cost of funds, often get beaten by small companies with their relatively high default risk and high cost of funds? The answer could be that small companies are more efficient with their scarce resources and can more quickly respond to market opportunities. For example, both Dell Computers and Gateway Computers became successful, innovative, high-growth companies and succeeded in a competitive computer industry against operating giants such as Compaq Computers, Digital Equipment, Wang Computers, IBM, and

---

1. There are companies that base their consulting practices on this approach, with one of the leading expert companies, Stern-Stewart, employing a proprietary economic value-added approach. This method has become very popular in the past decade in determining executive compensation.

Xerox.[2] Similarly, a start-up company, Southwest Airlines, used highly successful cost efficiencies and operating strategies to beat airline giants American, Delta, and United irrespective of high barriers to entry (high fixed and operating expenses) and traditionally tough market conditions.[3]

Small companies frequently beat major companies despite the long odds. Small companies can generate great business ideas, keep costs low, and generate high rates of return. But they often do not have access to risk capital. Perhaps, more important, they often have insufficient risk capital to carry them through all of the critical years until they make it to profitability.

Venture Financing Requires a "Portfolio Perspective"

The cash flows and financings of high-potential SEU ventures are very different from typical large company investments, but are presumed to be very similar to traditional capital venture projects or other high-potential ventures. High-potential ventures tend to have very low-to-negative cash flows in the early years, and then later hope to turn cash flow positive (i.e., profitable). Most individual investors would find this gamble too much risk to handle and would normally not invest in such types of projects or

---

2. In fact, our analysis of stockholder return for the period 1995–2000 showed that both Dell Computers and Gateway Computers provided one of the strongest growth rates among any of the publicly traded companies.

3. Legendary investor Warren Buffet once said "despite putting in billions and billions and billions of dollars, the net return to owners from being in the entire airline industry, if you owned it all, and if you put up all this money, is less than zero." Taken from a 1995 speech to students at the Kenan-Flagler Business School at the University of North Carolina at Chapel Hill, PBS Home Video, *Warren Buffet Talks Business*, 1999.

organizations if it were available to them.[4] This is one of the reasons why employees/entrepreneurs in SEUs should be entitled to an equity stake. Their risk is higher, so they should receive equity (or equity-like returns) to compensate for the additional risk in their new venture.

The cash flows in new ventures typically follow the appearance of a "J-curve" (shown in Figure 8.1). New ventures often lose money in the first few years (with the losses often increasing in the second and third years) and then become positive a few years later. If, during the low cash flow period, the project/firm does not get refinanced or an additional cash flow injection, the ballgame is over. At this stage the new company has nontransferable intellectual capital because its completion is incomplete and nearly impossible to get refinanced.

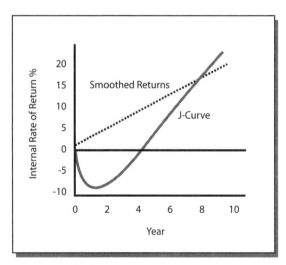

Figure 8.1 Cash flows from venture projects

---

4. As a practical matter, individual investors typically need to meet a "Qualified Investor" hurdle before being allowed to invest in VC funds. This requirement is based on an income or net worth threshold and is intended for sophisticated or high net worth investors (e.g., $200,000/$300,000 income for individual/married couple or $1,000,000 net worth).

This represents one of the reasons why up to 80% of all small businesses are estimated to go bankrupt within the first five years. Since the project/firm usually has a limited operating history and few credit-worthy assets, banks won't lend money. Consequently, if the venture capitalists or risk capital providers withhold future investments, or if the entrepreneurs/owners have limited personal capital to put into their company, the ventures will have insufficient funds to continue. New ventures often deplete their funds during this early, critical time and are forced to terminate their business.

Investors in SEU ventures should expect the same cash flows. This means that employees/entrepreneurs in the SEU venture should consider the personal/professional risks of being in a venture that may not be funded during the critical first three years of venture life. Their risk will be much higher in the SEU compared to the parent firm.

Institutional investors and other sophisticated or high net worth individuals recognize the risks inherent in high-potential new ventures and invest anyway. This is due to their portfolio perspective with investing in risky investments. Professional investors anticipate that only a few good investments in their portfolio will earn money. However, it is their expectation that their few good investments will earn more than enough return to compensate for the bad investments.

Traditionally, the rule of thumb with venture investments is that out of every 100 investment opportunities, a venture capitalist will typically select 1 or 2. For purposes of this illustration, let's assume 1. Then, out of every 10 investments (i.e., 1,000 investment opportunities), VCs will have a portfolio with approximately 6 or 7 that will either be complete duds or on death's doorstop (also known as "walking wounded"). From this same group of 10 investments, 2 to 3 will provide a modest rate of return and 1 or 2 will provide a very strong return or "home run." In a few cases a venture fund might experience a major "home run" investment that provides returns greater than 50 times original investment. Apple Computers, Intel, and Digital Equipment are examples of these. They more than compensated the risk capital provider for the losers and mediocre returns of the other investments.

However, the orientation for venture funds is much different than with traditional investments. With traditional investments, the investor expects each to provide at least some modest return, compared to the lopsided nature of venture investments (where most of the return comes from a small percentage of the projects). There are many other differences among the types of investments, with SEUs expected to follow a pattern similar to other venture fund projects.

- SEU venture companies will have little operating history

- SEU projects will require a higher degree of personal involvement

- SEU ventures will be illiquid investments (historically a 3-year + process)

- SEU ventures will be difficult to value (no public market)

- SEU ventures will generally require future rounds of financing

SEU ventures will be much riskier than the average investment made by a large, publicly held firm. This must be true almost by definition. If the investment or project had the same risk as all other big-company projects or investments, the company would simply fund the project through its normal capital budgeting process (approach toward funding long-life projects). These companies would evaluate the investment, assess the risk, and determine whether or not the risk warranted the investment. Large companies do this all the time. This is part of their traditional growth process and part of their existing R&D. A venture deal, such as an SEU, is different. A venture investment is typically performed in a new, unproven sector of the industry. The risks are higher, but so are the returns. It takes a certain mindset and discipline to handle this type of investment. Historically, large companies have not been very good at exploiting venture deals, but the potential, nevertheless, still exists. Part of the problem may be the manner in which large companies set up their funds. In particular, they often do not diversify in the same manner as professional investors.

Diversification: Different Ways to Reduce Risk

Most investors know a little something about diversification. The phrase "don't put all of your eggs in one basket" usually comes to mind. Certainly professional money managers and venture capitalists know all about diversification. Professional investors tend to live by this mantra, otherwise in one bad year they can be eliminated. But when it comes to venture investments in large corporations, sometimes market conditions and corporate policies limit all the different ways that venture funds can diversify. There are basically four different ways in which venture funds, including SEUs, can be diversified. These include the following.

1. Stage of Company Development: Venture investments in products or services can be divided into four distinct stages: (1) seed, idea, or start-up stage; (2) early stage or product development (beta testing); (3) expansion stage; and (4) later stage or pre-IPO. Managers of a venture fund can invest in different stages of company development to reduce the risk of the venture portfolio.

2. Industrial Sector: Venture investments can be diversified according to industrial sector. Although an organization with

a fund in one sector may not want to diversify in other sectors, the Facilitator might be able to bring in other third-party investors that would like to diversify into the SEU venture as part of a diversified portfolio. Common areas of interest for VC or risk investors have included: computer hardware/software, medical and health care, telephone and data communications, media, and biotechnology.

3. Geographical Region: Venture investments can be diversified based on geographic region. If there is a concentration in a certain geographical area (i.e., Silicon valley), the investor needs to gauge if he or she is comfortable with that bet and may look to other regions to reduce the risk of a venture portfolio.

4. Vintage Year: Diversification by vintage year is extremely important (discussed in greater length later). The vintage year refers to the year the funds were put to work. Because the holding period often averages three to seven years, it is important to stagger the fund investments and commitments over an extended period of time. Because VC funds typically follow a negative return in the early years (management fees and write-offs—classic "J" curve approach) it is important to have a long-term focus to carry the fund through to its successful completion. Otherwise, the fund can be destroyed in the early periods without a chance to recover.

Financiers or risk capital providers to SEU ventures do not need to follow each of these approaches. In fact, in some cases, such as the "industrial sector" category, risk capital providers may not want to invest outside certain industry classifications in which they do not have specific industry expertise. But they need to realize that by not diversifying in one of these areas that they have risk exposure to failure. Perhaps not surprisingly, the entrepreneur or fund recipient needs to think about these considerations as well. What happens if the funding agent has all (or most) of its liquid funding reserves dry up during the young firm's second year? What if the young firm is at its lowest point on the J curve? Unfortunately, many would-be dot.com success stories discovered the funding risk problems the hard way. During the 2000–2003 economic downturn, the risk capital market shrank by 50 to 75% and with it, the extra reserves to continue operations. Only the best organizations received the second- and third-stage rounds of financing. Many of the other venture projects shriveled up and disappeared.

SEU Ventures Need to be Diversified by Year of Investment

Big companies got into the venture market late (i.e., mid- to late-1990s) and many left it early (2000–2003). In essence, they bought into the market at the high end of the demand and pricing and may have bailed out at the low end. This becomes problematic as they were not able to diversify by the year of the investment. Given the poor cash flows of many large companies during the 2000–2003 time period, they couldn't. In many cases they were scrambling for funds to pay to meet existing operational needs, let alone new initiatives in high-risk venturing activities.

But a corporate venture fund generally requires a long-term approach. This is the approach that professional money managers and venture capitalists employ, even though corporate venture funds may not. Large companies, such as Lucent, Cisco, Nortel, Motorola, and Panasonic, created venture initiatives to take advantage of explosive growth in technology companies and new industry sectors. During the mid- to late-1990s, many of the corporate venture funds had a nearly limitless cash reservoir to tap for new initiatives. Further, many managers of the funds anticipated that future cash flows from the investment pool would be used to finance additional investments in the future. However, during the recession years 2000–2003, many of these corporate venture capitalists have since terminated their funds. In some cases, such as with Lucent, the firms have sold off all of their holdings and completely dismantled their venture group.[5]

Unfortunately, the portfolio investments went down at precisely the same time that the organization's primary business was faltering. Thus, any spare funds from the investments needed to be funneled back to the parent. There was no spare cash left over to put into new venture investments. Large company pension fund managers have learned how to deal with this same risk and now know how to invest in a manner so that the investments in company pension funds do not also decline at the same time as the corporate cash flows. Corporate venture funds for SEU investments will need to be handled in the same manner. This means that the investments in SEU ventures should be diversified by the year of investment. Moreover, because SEU ventures, unlike capital venture fund investments, are not geared toward a harvest, risk capital providers need to focus on the annual rate of return, rather than a one-time large cash distribution.

---

5. See, for example, "Lucent Sells Majority Stake in New Venture Unit," *EETimes,* January 4, 2002. Lucent sold an 80% stake of its New Ventures Group to Coller Capital. Celiant Corp. was among the 26 ventures that were bundled in this grouping for approximately $120 million. On February 19, 2002, Celiant was acquired by Andrew Corporation for $470 million (later reduced to approximately $390 M), see "Andrew Acquires Power Amp Supplier Celiant," *Site Management and Technology,* June 26, 2002.

SEU Ventures Do Not Focus on Harvest

Risk capital providers, such as venture capitalists, tend to focus on the harvest. As Figure 8.2 shows, the reasons should be clear. Venture capitalists only receive a financial windfall if they can achieve a harvest with a large distribution. But one of the big differences between investing in VC projects and SEUs is that SEUs are *not* set up with a harvest in mind. Consequently, the financial focus of SEUs should be geared toward the annual cash flows or return generated and not the cash distribution from a sale or harvest. This means that the risk capital financier that provides funds to a SEU needs to reevaluate the rules of success.

Venture capitalists derive their compensation from two central areas: capital commitment and capital gains on investments.

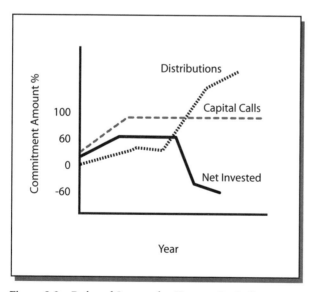

Figure 8.2   Rules of Success for Venture Capitalists

The first point addresses the total amount of funds that the risk provider has under management. Typically, the VC earns a 1 to 2% fee on the amount of the commitment from the investor (e.g., institutional investor like a pension fund, etc.)—not the amount invested. They earn their fees this way to prevent a moral hazard. If they earned fees on the amount of money invested they would have a bias toward making an investment, even a bad investment, just to earn their fees. This way they can pay for their overhead and operate as they should. The amount of the "capital call" represents how much the VC actually puts to work. As a practical matter, they often do not invest all of the money that is available (e.g., total capital commitment). They expect (and hope) that some money from prior investments will start to earn a return before the total capital commitment is exhausted.

The "real money" that venture capitalists earn comes from the harvest of deals. Venture capitalists usually have an 80/20 split. This means that they earn 20% of all gains, even though the vast majority of the capital invested in the project is not theirs. The capital comes from their investors (pension funds, high net worth individuals, etc.). Therefore, VCs have great incentive to see these deals work out well and provide an early harvest. The timing of the harvest depends on current market conditions and expectations of future growth. Generally, VCs are motivated to harvest as soon as possible. Harvest opportunities are very sensitive to market conditions and VCs are eager to lock in their profits given the chance. Thus, unless the venture shows extraordinary potential for explosive growth, VCs are inclined to cash out the first chance they get.

The *actual* returns on a VC fund demonstrate that the realized return on VCs is far less than the usual media hype of 40 to 70%

returns. In fact, the actual return performance has been in the 10 to 20% range.[6] The probability of high performance hinges almost exclusively on the "home run" investment. Venture returns are not uniformly distributed across investments. One half of the gains come from 7% of the investments (about 1 in 15). Moreover, diversification is important. Studies have shown that approximately one third of all investments lose money and one tenth to one sixth of all investments loses 100% of the funds invested. Clearly, these are not the typical returns for the average, individual investor.[7]

Figure 8.2 shows the bias toward getting to harvest. The venture capitalist can only earn big returns if the investments are harvested. Empirical evidence suggests that venture capitalists are good at timing the market. They know when to sell. Because most investments do not provide much, if any, return, the venture capitalist has tremendous incentive to harvest their investments earlier, rather than later in the development cycle. They might, and probably will, sacrifice some greater return in the future to achieve a good return in the short term. They would have to be highly confident that the returns in future years will be terrific to delay the harvest. They wouldn't want to risk a bad capital market to delay or possibly destroy altogether the possibility of harvest. This is one fundamental problem with the VC process.

In a venture capitalist's ideal scenario, after a few years the distributions (income returns and capital gains) start to exceed the original investment. This implies that the venture capitalist has received more money back from distributions than what they origi-

---

6. See, for example, Venture Economics' 1997 Investment Benchmarks Report.
7. See, for example, "Selecting and Structuring Investments: The Venture Capitalist's Perspective," by L. Gardella, *Readings in Venture Capital,* AIMR 1997; or, "Venture Capital," C. Barry, *Alternative Investing,* AIMR, 1998.

nally put into the total portfolio. They received all of their original money back plus some extra cash. This is their goal. They then scour the markets for their next investment opportunity.

SEU: Different Investment Orientation Focusing on Annual Return

Investments in SEUs will have a different orientation than investments in traditional venture fund portfolios. Because the intent of the SEU is not to harvest through a strategic sale or IPO, the venture should continue with a strategic link to the parent for a longer time period (compared to the average holding period with a normal VC investment). Consequently, the financial success or failure should be viewed in the context of the annual returns (or contribution toward large company profits) relative to the original investment. Although the early returns should be expected to be low (owing to the "J" curve effect), cash flow returns in later years should be relatively strong (particularly given a portfolio context). Thus, a portfolio of SEU investments should provide a steady stream of rising cash flow/dividends to the investor with a very strong annual return. Assuming that the cash flows of an SEU venture approach or exceed those of other corporate venturing or capital venture projects, the annual returns should be equally high (or higher) than the returns on other venture funds. The primary difference with this investment is that the investor should not expect the fund to be forced into liquidation after five to seven years, and the initial investment may be left in the SEU venture. However, as we discuss later, any risk capital investor that desires to receive liquidity for his, her, or their original investment will have an opportunity to convert the SEU stock into the stock of the parent company. Thus, the investor will be allowed liquidity in the SEU stock investment without forcing the SEU investment to liquidate.[8]

Big Firms Should Provide Risk Capital to Small Firms and Charge the Market Rate

Large, publicly traded organizations have access to cheap capital and have the ability to provide the capital to small, emerging companies at rates that are much lower than what these small companies could otherwise get. They also provide an opportunity to provide liquidity to investors in the SEU projects without forcing a sale or IPO. This presents an opportunity for both the large company and SEU venture. Large companies can act as a financial intermediary by taking their cheap capital from public and institutional investors and putting it to work where they have strategic insight by investing in SEUs. SEUs should pay the market rates for funds because this will encourage them to be selective with their spending. Moreover, market interest rates will reward the large company for its ability to act as a financial intermediary. The funds have an opportunity cost and the large firms are entitled to the benefits related to the risk capital they provide.

---

8. This liquidity versus liquidation comment is a subtle, yet important distinction. Given the traditional nature of VC investments, the stock holdings are virtually always privately held and do not provide the investor an opportunity to "pull out" the original investment or "liquidate" the holdings without a strategic sale or IPO. However, because SEU investments are set up with publicly traded companies, there is an opportunity to convert the stock of an SEU into the stock of the publicly traded parent organization. This allows the SEU to provide the investors or holders of equity an opportunity to gain "liquidity" of their holdings without forcing the company to sell or "liquidate" its organizational structure.

Large Companies Provide More than Just Cash—Catalysts for Growth

Large companies employ talented individuals with expertise in their industry. They can recognize new talent and a potentially valuable enterprise. Moreover, large companies have the power of production, distribution, and goodwill. These are invaluable traits that can assist a fledgling operation. Potentially, these attributes are even more valuable than the cash itself.

Small entrepreneurial companies know how to invest cash efficiently. At least this is probably a good filter for the successful ones. Given their relatively unstable cash flow and inability to generate excess cash, they need to operate with an eye on severe capital constraints and savvy resource management. These are skills often found lacking in a large organization with an abundance of capital. In fact, this may be one factor among many that distinguishes between a large and a small company. Small, successful entrepreneurial companies use expensive risk capital judiciously and keep their overhead costs very low.

Efficient Utilization Is More Important than Cost of Funds

The savings from using less capital will usually offset the higher cost per dollar used. Let's assume that a small company can use half the capital of a big firm but has to pay double the rate. The scenarios are not the same. As shown in Table 8.1, if a small company has to pay a 20% effective interest rate for its capital and only uses $1M of funding, it would use appreciably less total capital than a large firm requiring $2M in funding (double the

Table 8.1   Allocation Efficiency

	Small Firm	Large Firm	Optimal Scenario
Theoretical funds allocation	$1M	$2M	$1M
Theoretical cost of funds	20%	10%	10%
Total cost (funds + interest)	$1.2M	$2.2M	$1.1M

investment) with a 10% effective interest rate (half the rate). In this example, the small firm pays a total of $1.2M compared to the $2.2M that the large company would pay. Obviously, this illustrates an extreme example, but the message is nonetheless obvious. *Capital costs may be less of a factor than efficient utilization.* Further, if small companies can earn an equal or higher return on the investment compared to large companies, despite the higher cost of funds, then the best or optimal combination would provide the small company the funds at the large company rate. This would create an incremental return of $.1M ($1.1 vs. $1.2) for the small firm and be exactly half the total cost for the large firm ($1.1M vs. $2.2M).

If the small firm is in fact more efficient with its capital utilization and the large firm is able to attract risk capital at a lower rate, the best combination should be apparent. Large companies should bring cheap money to the small companies who can most efficiently put it to work. The small firm/large firm combination makes sense from both a theoretical and practical perspective.

Perfect Fit: Small Firm Growth Orientation; Large Firm Resources

In a perfect world (from a large company's perspective), the world's most efficient capital user would also be the company that has the best projects and the lowest cost of funds. This efficient model of an organization would grow larger, more efficient, and more profitable. These firms would become more powerful over time and dominate all others.

However, despite the implied advantages and access to inexpensive capital, large organizations fail to capitalize on their strategic advantage. The problem therefore has little to do with the cost of funds and perhaps more to do with its successful allocation. Who gets the funds and how efficiently is this process handled?

Large companies need a better way to distribute their inexpensive risk capital. They have a clear advantage over other firms in this regard and need to utilize funds in an efficient, cost-effective manner. Either they will need to spend money with a cost-conscious orientation or they will need to allocate funds to a small group that already has this inherent view. Because the former might require a complicated corporate culture overhaul, the latter becomes a more pragmatic approach.

Large companies should continue with experimentations in small venture financings. Moreover, they should invest the funds as professional fund managers and apply a portfolio context so that they are fully diversified based on timing of distribution, risk of venture opportunity, geographic representation, and (wherein possible) industrial allocation. The basic concept for venture financing is already readily accepted within most major companies, but the existing approach requires some modifications. Large companies should continue to partner with many small companies and provide their cheap capital to those that can make them both a profit.

Capital allocations will need a slightly different risk-return oriented approach with different incentives for the members of the venture. The focus will be geared toward annual returns from the investments rather than a large cash distribution or harvest. Further, this will encourage long-term thinking by members of the SEU ventures and participating stakeholders. The SEU format should also assist large organizations with appropriate allocations of its scarce resources.

9

LIQUIDITY VERSUS LIQUIDATION: CASHING OUT OF THE SEU

Harvest Without Selling

For many business owners and other stakeholders, nothing is more important than the harvest. A harvest means that owners cash out of their venture. This is where equity holders sell their businesses or go public through an IPO after many years of hard labor and personal sacrifice. For some owners and stakeholders a good harvest is not just the most important thing—it is the only thing. The harvest becomes all-encompassing, all-consuming. It drives daily human behavior toward a common purpose culminating in a financial windfall.

The reason for individual focus should be clear: the harvest is usually the biggest part of an individual's lifetime compensation. In fact, many individuals will have sufficient wherewithal to retire. They will never need to work again. Others besides owners benefit too. For example, dealmakers require a harvest to earn their commission and have enormous economic incentive to see it through completion.[1] If a harvest doesn't transpire, then the dealmakers can lose their invested energy and time, and might also be out-of-pocket for considerable costs in preparation of a deal. Thus, they will exert great energy to push a company through a strategic sale, IPO, or consolidation. This might be true even if the harvest is incompatible with the organizational direction and focus and is detrimental to long-term value creation. Harvests should be accomplished at a time that is beneficial to the deal—not necessarily to the participants in the deal.

The SEU template does not allow third-party financiers to drive the timing or mechanism of harvest but does create economic incentive for them to participate in a venture. Further, the SEU does not force external financiers or small equity holders (e.g., minority owners) to permanently own stock they cannot cash out. There is a big difference between "cashing out" and liquidating the entire venture to meet the same goal. In the first case, stakeholders simply want liquidity or access to their funds whereas in the latter case, the venture or assets need to be sold to meet the same purpose. The SEU template, as it is applied with a large company, can easily meet the "harvest" needs of third-party financiers without disrupting the value creation motivation.

---

1. For example, in the case of the Daimler Chrysler merger, Goldman Sachs received a reported $65 million in fees, whereas CS First Boston received approximately $55 million, Levy Zuckerman, "Merger Mayhem," *Bloomberg Magazine*, October, 1998.

Harvest Focuses Energy

There are few situations in an organizational existence that bring out the commonality of purpose like an upcoming IPO. Employees help prepare the books and "road show" for investment presentations to prospective investors and the media place the company in the spotlight. Through an IPO, stakeholders in the company have instant liquidity of their holdings. They can spend this money any way they chose, or set it aside for retirement. In many cases a "hot IPO" appreciates the stock price considerably, sending net worth holdings soaring along with discretionary consumption (e.g., expensive homes, cars, jewelry, vacations). Consequently, an IPO may even benefit those who don't own a direct stake in the public venture (i.e., brokers, retail sales, etc.). IPOs are a harvest mechanism that creates excitement and wealth for many. However, as we've seen in the 2000–2003 recession, when markets turn, they can change very quickly. Many of the "hot IPOs" from 1997 to 2000 went bankrupt a few years later and operations ceased to exist.

Companies may also harvest through a strategic sale or consolidation (M&A). This situation also grabs the attention of company stakeholders, but in a different manner than an IPO. With an IPO, fresh capital enters the company to fuel future expansion of an existing management team; in the case of a strategic sale, many management and employment changes may occur. This may create apprehension among workers who are each trying to protect their jobs. Sometimes situations occur (i.e., turf battles or corporate politics), to the detriment of long-term growth, as members scramble for scarce resources.

Harvests create both passion and uneasiness, but they do not necessarily create long-term wealth. Problems may ensue if incentives are built into businesses that encourage individuals to focus on harvest considerations rather than long-term value creation. Key long-term stakeholders need to carefully rethink the individual motivations and incentives offered by the business if they want to effectively grow and build an enterprise over a long period of time. One of the most important problems related to the harvest is that some individuals, who clearly have a short-term economic motivation, have the ability to push the new venture toward a deal.

Financiers Need a "Harvest"

Financiers do not reap their rewards until they achieve a harvest. This means they are single-mindedly focused on the harvest event. Some financiers, such as venture capitalists, don't even enter a deal without a harvest strategy in mind. They carefully think through the path of growth and various combinations that will enable them to accomplish a harvest in their allotted time period.

Venture capitalists and investment bankers are adept at putting together deals. They know how to sell the deal to management and other stakeholders by stressing a laundry list of benefits including: cost reductions, revenue enhancement, economies of scale, asset consolidation, executive leadership, vision for the future, stock price increase, and legacy. In the past, those within the company that opposed a consolidation would typically lose. Senior management and other key stakeholders had economic incentive to form a larger company (pay rises with size of firm) and were inclined to acquiesce to the opinions of external experts. This was particularly true if significant benefits were claimed to be forthcoming.

However, the evidence of the M&As of the 1990s demonstrated that many M&A deals did not create value for shareholders. In fact, in the short term dealmakers prospered, yet few other stakeholders did. The single-minded focus of the harvest became a big problem.

Over the years, venture capitalists and investment bankers have earned their share of accolades for all of the good that they contributed to our society's economic development. But this does not absolve them from their share of the responsibility during the crazed telecom and dot.com era. They certainly contributed to the spiraling greed environment during the 1995–2000 period. Their contributions to this equation centered on harvesting deals irrespective of whether or not it was in the long-term interests for all other stakeholders. By the time the financial markets finally realized that the combinations were not working well, it was already too late. Stocks plummeted and perceived value from the combinations evaporated. Former dealmakers were no longer involved and shareholders and management turned their attention to organizational survival.

Lessons Learned

What were the lessons learned during this period? How can long-term investors ensure that this pattern is not repeated? In some respects the market mechanism corrects itself, as evidenced with reduced M&A activity in the early 2000s. But institutional memory tends to be short. In a few years newly minted MBAs will enter the arena with new answers to old questions. Just as their predecessors, they too may ignore the mistakes of the prior generation. History can repeat itself given the right mix of market conditions. The odds of this pattern increase as long as our organizational infrastructures and market mechanisms operate in the same manner. Our incentive systems and harvest mechanisms are a big part of the infrastructure. Risk capital providers, dealmakers, and corporate executives will not likely change their behavior as long as the policies continue unchanged and regulators do not force them to perform otherwise. They'll continue to operate under the well-established rules that all others follow.

Change to the system will not occur automatically. After all, those who have the ability to change the rules are also among those who receive the greatest short-term benefit when the market returns to its customary routines. Modifications to old habits will require a different mindset and orientation. This especially holds true as it relates to compensation and incentive mechanisms associated with harvests. In the recent past, there was too much economic incentive to complete a deal, rather than complete the "right" deal. In retrospect, the best course of action may have been to make no deal at all and perhaps look for an alternative approach to provide financiers with liquidity.

The SEU template bypasses the focus on harvest by creating liquidity for investors through the large company's publicly traded stock. This allows the SEU to grow without unnecessary disruptions associated with "cashing out" key stakeholders. Moreover, by minimizing M&A activity, external transactions costs will be low and corporate infighting (associated with consolidations) will be reduced. Only transactions that actually create long-term efficiencies will be pursued, and therefore should only include those companies classified as "appropriate corporate fit."

Value Creation Sometimes Takes Time

Value creation is not a simple matter. Some companies take a while to reach full potential. Intel, Microsoft, and Dell Computers are all examples of companies that have continued to develop organic growth and value over long periods of time. Krispy Kreme Donuts is an example of a company that took 60 years to mature before reaching full potential (founded in 1937).

Quality ventures need time to develop and grow. They need time to bring together the proper talent and they need time to allow all value-creating parties to develop to their full potential. The harvest should not drive the development. Value should be created naturally, through a template that fosters maximum contribution from as many value-creating parties as humanly possible. It should not be driven by the dealmakers. These people are good at determining the value or maybe even exchanging the value, but usually not the people creating new products, processes, or distribution channels.

The people that create long-term value include scientists in the laboratories or employees that meet with customers. Value creators may also be employees in the manufacturing plant or administrative offices who dream of new products and new solutions to meet the needs of the marketplace. These people see the possibilities for handling business in a different, more efficient manner. Their timetable does not necessarily coincide with harvest opportunities, but certainly needs to be sensitive to market conditions. Letting the availability of a harvest drive long-term value creation is the equivalent of letting the tail wag the dog.

Through the past 30 to 40 years financial experts and management consultants applied all types of innovations in creating value through financial or accounting sophistry. Many of these approaches offered quick fixes to complex problems. Some were just fads.

In the 1960s and 1970s, management used corporate acquisitions for diversification. Later, in the 1980s and early 1990s, firms focused on "core" or "strategic value" and implemented corporate divestitures and equity carve-outs (selling of parts of company) for pure play scenarios. They experimented with "financial engineering," which included a fancy way to acquire cheap debt by securing loans with strong collateral (i.e., "securitization" or "collateralization" of assets). During this era, management buyouts (MBOs) and leveraged buyouts (LBOs) became popular, in which management tried to buy out public shareholders through heavy debt loads. Sometimes takeovers became hostile and were embroiled in public bidding wars or litigation. Through the early- to mid-1990s management pursued "roll-ups" and leveraged buildups in which companies grew through horizontal mergers (mergers across similar industries) or consolidation. This was an old idea for garnering economies of scale, but they often didn't meet expectations. Toward the end of the century we witnessed unprecedented M&A and IPO transactions coinciding with corporate venturing activity. The stock markets and company valuations appreciated considerably, irrespective of revenues or cash flows.

In the post dot.com era, financial markets are once again focusing on strategic fit and cash flow generation. Investment analysts are once again scrutinizing the applications of cash raised in an IPO and why companies should be strategically aligned. Attention is now being placed into how value is being created after the funds are raised and how they are being put back to work in operations. Given the experience of the 1990s, financial transactions need to be justified as to how they will create value.

Stakeholders in SEUs do not worry about harvesting due to market conditions. If they have been set up as a strategic play with a large corporate affiliation, the timing of the harvest becomes irrelevant. Stakeholders in SEU ventures have economic and personal incentive to stay focused on building value through long-term strategic orientations without concern in regard to harvest conditions. For some stakeholders, the SEU venture may represent a life-time achievement and they will be hardworking and loyal to the venture regardless of market and harvest considerations. They will likely have a long-term "owner's mentality."

SEUs Shift Orientation to an Owner's Mindset

Individuals who work for others often don't experience an "owner's mentality." There is nothing wrong with this approach; most people don't want the burdens associated with ownership and work for someone else. Ownership comes with financial risk, responsibility, and commitment. There is a lot of work associated with owning a business. There is great payoff and satisfaction too. Furthermore, owners develop a business that usually appreciates in value over time. Owners can borrow funds against the equity in their business or pass the equity value in their business to family and friends. Perhaps more important, business owners have control. They can hire, fire, and make business decisions. Ultimately, good business decisions are their reward and bad business decisions cost them money. They have an equity stake in a business that after a lifetime's achievement is probably worth something. Maybe it represents all that they have accomplished in life. In many cases, the business survives them long after they are gone.

SEUs create an opportunity for entrepreneurs to experience an owner's mentality. Sure, individuals can own equity in a large company through direct stock purchase or through stock options, but an SEU ownership stake is different. *Owning equity in a business is not the same as owning a business.* Employees at large, public firms can accumulate equity in their parent company. They do not own

the company. It's not even close. For most workers at a large organization the contributions are either insignificant or unrelated to
their daily chores. Their equity accumulation really amounts to
more of an appreciating/depreciating bonus pool. It rarely ties to a
vested equity stake in a personal venture. Moreover, with increasing pressures from ERISA (the professional retirement agency overseeing pension funds), there is a greater likelihood for pension fund
managers to diversify employee assets *away* from the parent's
stock—not toward it. Thus, large company employees will hold a
more diversified portfolio of stock holdings but feel less connected
with the success and sufferings of the parent. With an SEU venture,
entrepreneurs can make a big difference and feel very much connected with the success and failures of the venture.

The SEU approach in this regard is not unlike classic corporate
venturing models. In these situations, risk capital providers like to
see the agents or entrepreneurs of the firm sweat a little bit during
the tough times. Financiers to a high-risk venture know that entrepreneurs who have an economic stake in the success of a venture
will work harder and smarter to ensure that they do not lose their
entire company or life's accomplishment. Owners in SEUs operate
in a similar manner.

Employees do not typically worry about the success of a venture,
unless it puts their job security at risk. Because they don't receive any
of the direct rewards of ownership they don't usually worry about
stock price returns (except for their ownership stake) or company
profits (unless their bonus is tied to this metric). If they can earn
more elsewhere they might leave. They have few worries, responsibility, and loyalty. These problems are the domain of owners.

SEUs, on the other hand, infuse owners with a sense of accomplishment and pride as they build value in their venture related to
their direct efforts. They have the responsibilities and long-term

owner's mentality, common in small, independent ventures. Large companies do not often experience this type of worker—but they could. It simply requires more developments like an SEU structure and providing entrepreneurs/stakeholders an opportunity to "cash out" without forcing a liquidation of the corporate assets.

Liquidity Is More Important than Harvest

The harvest is a terrific mechanism for participating individuals to achieve a fair market value in their equity holdings and to receive liquidity. But, a harvest doesn't mean that individuals will necessarily spend all of their money once they receive it. In fact, far from spending their cash, individuals participating in the harvest are likely to save it. Individuals often spend some of the money from their harvest, but then treat the balance as a retirement fund or a cash reservoir. The harvest reflects many years of hard work and sacrifice; they will be reluctant to squander such efforts in an immediate burst of spending. So why do people experience a sensation in participating with a harvest? If all they are doing is moving their assets from one account to another, why is there such jubilation? Their net worth hasn't really changed.

The answer is that their funds are now liquid and they are free to spend them whenever they need them and on whatever purpose that serves them. Prior to the harvest, their equity may have had an estimated market value on paper, but it was just that—a theoretical estimate. There was always some risk that the deal would not be realized or that the value would drop before the funds could be tapped. Equity could disappear along with any dreams of future consumption. However, once funds are realized in a harvest, the amount becomes known and can be placed in a bank, mutual fund, or Treasury securities. This is an important distinction. A harvest recognizes and *realizes* liquid, economic value. This means that instead of holding illiquid stock where the holder is uncertain about the value, stockholders have cash or an asset that can be easily converted into a known amount of cash.

Liquidity with an SEU Couldn't Be Easier

Providing liquidity to entrepreneurs within an SEU associated with a large multinational organization couldn't be easier. The SEU is already affiliated with a public organization. Years earlier the large company performed an IPO and now has public stock holdings actively traded on a major stock exchange. Publicly traded stock provides a very useful, convenient currency.

Gaining liquidity in an SEU venture couldn't be simpler. The key requirement is calibrating the value of the SEU venture and then converting it into the parent company's publicly traded stock. Consequently, the problems associated with new venture liquidity, an overwhelmingly significant issue for most ventures, are not and should not be an issue with SEUs affiliated with large, publicly traded organizations. Large companies bring liquidity for SEU participants to the bargaining table. This is an extraordinarily powerful feature. This has powerful repercussions on the growth and development of new ventures as well as the type of entrepreneurs and financiers that may be attracted to working on a corporate venture with the large, public company. SEU ventures partnered with large, publicly traded organizations are not dependent on the state of financial markets or the determination of financiers when the company should be harvested. This is a major advantage. Because large, publicly traded organizations can provide liquidity to individuals on an "anytime basis," the need to set up the venture for the sake of a harvest diminishes. In fact, by reducing the emphasis on harvest, companies will save considerable transaction fees as well as the energies associated with the preparations of a deal.

Fewer Harvests Means Lower Fees and More Focused Energies

Harvesting a venture can be very expensive. Not only do companies pay a percentage of the deal cost (approaching 10% for small deals), they divert considerable institutional energy making preparations for external buyers or investors. Senior management might be diverted for months, focusing on a harvest or preparing the company for an intensive due diligence inspection.

Harvesting an SEU venture through a public stock conversion with the parent is different. It does not require investment bankers to prepare a "road show" and does not require extensive due diligence by external parties.[2] It does not require a strategic sale (though benchmarking the value would be helpful) and does not require a venture capitalist to force an early conversion (due to a hot market). Small SEU ventures with a public company can easily convert their equity into the parent's stock cheaply and efficiently. Moreover, because the parent already has publicly traded stock, the entrepreneurs in the SEU venture may be further benefited by converting private stock into much more valuable public stock.

---

2. A "road show" is the term applied to the process of investment bankers showcasing management talent in front of prospective institutional investors (i.e., portfolio managers).

Private to Public Conversion Creates Instant Value!

SEUs that harvest through a public market conversion with the parent have another huge advantage. In addition to establishing immediate market value, gaining liquidity, and saving transaction fees, by converting private stock into public stock the holder receives a security, which has considerably greater value. Academic studies show that moving from privately held to publicly held stock increases the value by about 60 to 70%![3] For example, as shown in Figure 9.1, the value of an enterprise increases by approximately 67% (shown as $3.60 to $6.00) when it moves from a minority position (not holding controlling interest) to a position with marketability (liquidity). Consequently, even if the company doesn't do anything else different, simply by converting from a privately traded stock to a publicly traded stock, the increase in liquidity makes the enterprise worth more money. It is worth appreciably more because investors value the opportunity to get rid of their investment quickly at fair market value. This is another way of describing liquidity.

Figure 9.1 shows an additional premium earned if the individual maintains control of an organization. This is a separate issue that is worth about the same amount as the change in liquidity. However, it is relevant for demonstrating that individuals place a premium price on being able to control the destiny of their own venture. This is the owner's mindset we referred to previously. It is worth a lot of money and participants in an SEU venture enjoy this benefit. As the figure shows, it is worth up to an additional 67%.

---

3. See, for example, "Minority Interest Discounts, Control Premiums, and Other Discounts and Premiums" (Chapter 14) or "Discounts for Lack of Marketability" (Chapter 15) in *Valuing a Business: The Analysis and Appraisal of Closely Held Companies,* Pratt, Reilly and Schweihs, Irwin, 1995.

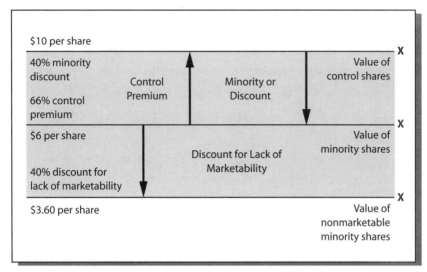

Figure 9.1   Control Premiums, Minority and Marketability Discounts

Entrepreneurs, in an SEU venture who can convert their holdings into a parent's actively traded public stock are extremely lucky. This opportunity brings together the best of both worlds. SEU participants can enjoy liquidity whenever they require funds, yet can still maintain a controlling interest (or significant stake) in their venture. Furthermore, the parent has a strategic alliance with participants that have a long-term incentive to grow their venture, which may likely appreciate at a faster rate than the parent's underlying stock.

SEU Value Does Not Depend on Appreciation of Parent's Stock

The parent's stock is merely being used for conversion purposes. Participants to the privately held ventures desire liquidity in their equity holdings—not necessarily the asset (i.e., parent's stock) that is being used for conversion. The value of the venture should not rest on the rise or fall of the parent's stock. In fact, providing SEU participants stock issues in the parent's stock might be counterproductive. Hopefully, the entrepreneurial venture will rise, regardless of the parent's performance. Given the small, focused nature of the SEU venture, it should rise at a faster rate than the parent.

The value of the venture should depend on independent appraisal and its own cash-flow generation, not the same market metrics used to value the parent organization. In an ideal situation, the venture would be benchmarked against other independent ventures not affiliated with the parent. Whereas influences related to industry conditions cannot keep the relationship completely unrelated to the parent, the important point is that the value of the entrepreneurial venture is determined though separate valuation procedures. The option to convert the private stock into public stock just represents the ability to harvest. It provides currency and peace of mind to the participants. It provides an ongoing benchmarked value and an ability to gain liquidity and financial independence. It provides an "owners mentality" without really costing the parent anything more.

Once the entrepreneurs in the SEU convert into the parent's stock, they have a separate consideration. At that point the entrepreneurs have to decide whether or not they want to hold a significant part of their net worth in a single stock (parent's) or trade it into something else. Tax, portfolio, and personal consumption considerations now enter the equation. Because the entrepreneurs no longer have control of the venture after conversion (i.e., small holdings of the parent's stock vs. large holding of their own private venture), they would be wise to diversify their holdings. Most financial advisors would encourage these people to sell their holdings in the parent company's stock and buy other securities. The conversion from private to public stock will have accomplished its purpose. They entrepreneurs will have earned their liquidity and can now manage their portfolio as they would any other windfall receipt.

Slight Twist to an Old Approach

Large, public organizations have a huge advantage compared to all other operating entities. However, the largest multinational organizations are not even coming close to tapping their full potential. These entities have actively traded public stock and the cheapest debt and equity capital available on the planet. They have great advantages to fuel future growth. Moreover, the publicly traded stock that these companies possess provides a unique currency that can be invaluable to other affiliated stakeholders. SEUs can convert their privately traded stock into a parent company's stock providing liquidity without the costs associated with a harvest. Moreover, by converting private stock into public stock, SEUs enjoy greater value in the conversion of their stock.

Traditionally, the focal point for many stakeholders participating in a high-potential venture has been the harvest. However, the advantage of a harvest is largely a determination of fair market value and establishing liquidity. This becomes an unnecessary exercise for a publicly traded company. The harvest should not be driven by market conditions or self-centered pursuits. Rather, the company should be allowed to grow with entrepreneurial partners (EntrePartneurs) maintaining a strong interest over a long period of time.

In the past, corporate venture models periodically provided a direct equity stake in the new venture or provided large corporate stock options in the parent for successful performance. However, in the former case the venture was forced into a strategic sale or IPO to create liquidity. In the latter case, the correlation with corporate stock options may have provided a security that had performance unrelated to the performance of the new venture creation.

The SEU template offers a slight modification to prior corporate venturing approaches. This approach minimizes transaction fees and takes advantage of the added value and liquidity associated with the parent company's stock. Offering company stock in lieu of value created or exceptional performance is certainly not a new concept. However, providing an equity stake that becomes valued independent of the parent's market metrics and building it into a conversion template for an SEU in lieu of an alternative harvest methodology is a slightly different twist to an old compensation dilemma. Large, public companies already have all of the pieces in place to implement this specific strategy.[4]

---

4. As a practical matter, many companies used company stock as currency for transactions. For example, Lucent Technologies used company stock to buy back corporate ventures that were being harvested in an open auction. In 1999, Lucent's Optical Networking Group (ONG) purchased Lucent Digital Video (LDV) from its new ventures group. ONG purchased LDV in an open auction by paying the highest price. Members within LDV had equity and were able to liquidate their holdings immediately or convert into Lucent stock.

10

WHERE DO WE GO FROM HERE? JUMPSTARTING THE PROCESS OF CHANGE

Large companies can no longer afford to run businesses as in the past. The fast, easy growth through M&A activity no longer continues. But companies need now, perhaps more than ever, new ways to enhance revenues and profits. No single path holds all of the answers. And rarely will any single path please all stakeholders.

But some approaches may be better than others. Some aspects from existing controversies will likely influence organizational models of the future. Disclosures of potential conflicts of interests, particularly as they relate to compensation and fees, will likely become more commonplace. Stakeholder (and especially management) actions will become more transparent and capitalizing on the system

179

for personal gain will become more difficult. These are probably healthy changes for institutions.

The SEU approach enables entrepreneurs who create value for the organization to be recipients of the wealth they create. This approach has been attempted by some large organizations in the past, but in a slightly different manner. This section describes how corporate officers can begin to implement these changes and raises a number of practical issues. For example, how should ambitious entrepreneurs within the organization approach senior officers without sending the wrong signal and how should outsiders partic-ipate in these new ventures? Further, do the SEU models of entre-preneurial venturing apply only to publicly held companies or could extensions of these models apply to privately held organiza-tions or nonprofit/governmental institutions as well?

This section presents a Question-and-Answer format to some of the more pressing problems in developing and implementing an SEU venture. Although there are limitations in addressing only a small sample of inquiries, this section offers some insights in how to initiate the new template with existing resource and institutional constraints.

One of the most difficult challenges in implementing an SEU may be in gathering institutional support and rallying stakeholder sup-port within the company. However, under the assumption that senior management has decided to embark on a new growth initiative, the following question-and-answer section describes ways in which organizational members can help contribute to this development.

Q: Does the SEU template apply to all companies?

A: No. There are many companies in which this template does not apply. First, if a company already has a successful ven-turing arm or growth model, there will be no incentive or rationale for change. Further, if the corporate culture is char-acterized by reluctance to change or embrace a new tem-plate, there is no opportunity to implement an SEU concept.

Q: Are some corporate cultures better for an SEU implementation than others? What characteristics may be common in entrepreneurial organizations that will help implement significant corporate change?

A: The way a firm is organized and structured greatly influences how it will address a separate venture. Organizations that are centered on distinct business units may be inclined to let a new venture operate independently (i.e., on its own). By contrast, a company with highly centralized functional units may want to force conformity upon all of its new ventures. Centralized organizations do not naturally like things to be different within the firm. Moreover, the larger the firm, the greater the danger that the various corporate staff members will want to become involved with the venture. It will require a strong "hands-off" order from the top, preferably a watchful CEO, to keep the corporate bureaucrats at bay. We identify a few characteristics that we believe will help distinguish between entrepreneurial and traditional organizations in Table 10.1.

Table 10.1 Characteristics that Distinguish between Entrepreneurial and Traditional Organizations

Factor	Entrepreneurial	Traditional
Organizational structure	Business units	Centralized
Culture/history	Team oriented	Bureaucratic
Leadership	Strong champion	Distant/remote
Venture history	Experimental	None
Human resources policies	Flexible	Rigid/uniform
Compensation	Individual goals	Corporate goals
Outsourcing degree	High	In-house bias
Finance control	Local control	Central staff
Founder role	Still involved	Professional management
CEO tenure	> 5 years	< 5 years

Q: How should the large company get started?

A: Change really begins at the top. If an SEU venture has any hope of surviving, the CEO must mandate the development of such a venture and help develop a basic template that identifies the scope, responsibilities, equity distribution, compensation, intellectual property, funding, and organizational control parameters. In the absence of CEO participation, and institutional independence, the SEU may be subject to the whims of economic instability or power changes within the organization. The CEO and his or her team need to decide the overall purpose of venturing. The ultimate purpose varies depending on whether it is for strategic growth, market expansion, product innovation, or product development.

Q: How important is corporate culture to the new venture's success?

A: Although the external business and environmental conditions may seem like obvious factors to even the casual observer, the internal factors are equally important and probably more difficult to forecast. Many entrepreneurs simply cannot survive in a rigid corporate climate. Consequently, they tend not to be attracted to working within the large, organizational infrastructure. Moreover if they do happen to find their way into the large, bureaucratic organization, they may not survive very long within it. The "wrong" corporate culture can be lethal to new venture creation and development. Selecting the right entrepreneurial partner may be difficult on its own. Making sure that the entrepreneur is protected and allowed to flourish without corporate interference may be another. The internal corporate business factors are central to new venture growth development. A few of the key factors are shown in Table 10.2.

Table 10.2   Internal Corporate Business Climate Factors

Organizational structure	Human relations policies
Corporate culture and history	Compensation
Leadership	Degree of outsourcing
Venturing history	Financial control
Founder role/CEO tenure	

Q: If the informal corporate culture is against change, is the new venture doomed?

A: If the firm has a history of embracing cross-functional use of personnel and is oriented around work teams, it may be more inclined to favorably accept a "renegade" venture being started than would a traditional situation. Conversely, if the corporate culture is steeped in hierarchical bureaucracy, it will probably spurn new forays or methodologies. Acceptance within the informal culture of the parent firm is critical to the new venture's success. If the corporate bureaucrats see the new start-up as a potential threat to their power and/or future, they may openly (or deceitfully) campaign against the new venture to preserve their power base. Management needs to recognize this potential threat and to work hard to reduce the internal anxiety that may be present. It cannot ignore the informal structure with its collective "heads in the sand."

On the other hand, proactive use of the informal structure will probably help the venture to succeed. Enthusiastic support and able volunteers can reduce corporate overhead and provide assistance and expertise that otherwise would be hard or expensive for the venture to procure. But the informal culture support does not occur by accident. Seasoned management knows that the best type of informal support is the result of careful planning and forethought. This is where leadership arises. Senior management, including the CEO, must strongly endorse the venture project and champion its cause. If management ignores the informal market, personnel at the new venture will be left vulnerable to the forces that want to grab hold or influence it. Of all the factors, proactive senior management support is vital to the success of the venture. This is true both in its initial phase and as the new venture matures.

Q: Does the corporate culture change over time and does the size or age of the venture influence its willingness to embrace a new concept?

A: Yes, corporate culture changes over time. Many large, public companies that are now sluggish and bureaucratic were dynamic entrepreneurial companies in their early days.

Where possible, it is helpful to maintain the energy and spirit that founders bring to their organizations. A survey of founder-managed, large companies suggests that the influence of the founder may be extremely helpful in maintaining the growth and spirit of the large company. For example, Bill Gates (Microsoft), Larry Ellison (Oracle), Michael Dell (Dell Computers), and Andy Grove (Intel) are all situations in which the founder/CEO stayed involved in the organization for a long period of time. Although many factors contribute to organizational growth, certainly a major factor is the vision and presence of a strong leader. Professional management needs to be careful about the decay of entrepreneurial spirit over time.

Q: *Members at our organization are eager to implement growth and change but are wrestling with the speed and scope of any new initiative. What are the advantages of small initiatives over large ones?*

A: The primary approach of the SEU encourages a portfolio of small, limited scope and focused ventures, rather than large and complex ones. The argument centers on the notion that it is easier to grow a small venture at a faster pace compared to a larger firm. However, because senior management probably does not have the time to filter and support a number of small firms, the SEU template recommends a third-party Facilitator to assist with deal flow, negotiations, and support. Large companies will still continue with significant strategic bets or investments. However, the SEU approach enhances diversification in new venture creation and sheds organizational burden (i.e., Facilitator) to those who can better handle these responsibilities.

Q: *Which comes first—the team, idea, or entrepreneur?*

A: Jeff Timmons from Babson College (previously at Harvard Business School) describes the creation of value being a combination of team, resources, and opportunity. Clearly, trying to create value in the absence of any of these attributes will be difficult. More important, it is necessary within any large organization to ensure that corporate management does not attempt to control or run the venturing process. The large organization should allow the Entrepreneur to build his or her team. Moreover, where possible the risk/reward ratio should attempt to match real-world levels. If people within the organization refuse to engage in the risk of external entrepreneurs (i.e., similar investment and salary consequences), they should be reminded (by an external party) that the returns should consequently be less significant as well.

Q: Where should the entrepreneurial talent come from—inside the firm or outside?

A: The question of where to look for talent is a common dilemma. Some large organization managers believe that there exists a self-selection bias or clientele effect within the firm. That is to say that they think true entrepreneurial talent would never even apply for a job at a large organization, much less work for one. This would suggest going exclusively outside for entrepreneurial talent. We actually believe that the optimal strategy is to look both inside and outside the firm. Too often companies either let the entrepreneur do all of the selection from outside, or go to the other extreme and staff it completely from inside. Neither way may, by itself, optimize the knowledge of internal politics and available resources from the inside, and the hungry enthusiasm and cost-conscious approach from the outside.

Q: Who should get this process started?

A: After the CEO decides to move forward with an SEU template, the large organization needs to identify the internal corporate champion. The corporate champion should be a senior executive within the parent firm that can manage the large company resources and keep the corporate politics away from the new ventures. This step is necessary to make sure that interfaces with the parent company are managed and that someone can "call off the dogs" within the company that may seek to force compliance. The champion should be named early in the process so that he or she can monitor the progress and be involved. This internal champion can also be the liaison with external parties and with the SEU Facilitator.

Q: How should future projects be funded?

A: The organization needs to allocate some risk capital for new venture creation or be comfortable with external funding coming from the outside. Clearly the funding will be critical to the success of the new ventures. The SEU model allows partial funding from the parent firm, but also enables funding to come from a variety of sources including: third-party investors, banks, and possibly venture capitalists. The SEU model suggests that VC funding be kept to a minimum because these parties usually like to control the final harvest scenario (which the SEU model doesn't provide). The SEU template does not allow a financier to dictate the type or timing of a harvest decision because it may be detrimental to the long-term development of the new venture.

Q: How can external parties get involved with an SEU project with a large company?

A: The SEU model provides considerable opportunity for entrepreneurs to partner with large companies. Entrepreneurs might be both inside and outside the firm. In particular, a large company might currently have untapped projects or projects they deem "ugly ducklings" that could be managed by outside talent. During periods of economic contraction it is possible, and perhaps even probable, that the large company might welcome an external party to assist with value creation and venturing on projects that they no longer have funding to complete or manage properly. Moreover, during periods of employee layoffs, venturing might create an alternative path for both the firm and the employee. Organizations should look for outsiders not to help solve their problems, but rather, to provide an additional source of revenue with relatively low effort and risk. So long as the firm has a facility in place to help generate this additional income, with external parties that will help negotiate terms and keep management's primary focus on important day-to-day operations, all parties gain.

Q: How should large organizations compensate their entrepreneurial people?

A: Clearly, one of the most contentious and poorly handled areas within the large organization relates to individual accounting and compensation. Many of the problems involved with organizational and security scandal/impropriety deal with individual compensation. Large organizations are accustomed to paying people in general categories (often referred to as "buckets"). Except for variable or incentive-based individuals (i.e., salespeople), the only individuals that tend to negotiate special compensation packages include senior executives. Otherwise, the large organization will have a Herculean task trying to manage all of the combinations and permutations involved with appropriateness and fairness. Large companies need to move to a system that allows more variable compensation with members at all levels within the organization. Moreover, they need to provide a mechanism that invites external members into the family of networks and affiliates. Only through creative compensation facilities will organizations be able to fill this strategic gap. The EntrePartneur process (discussed earlier) establishes variable compensation within an SEU framework. Using an SEU Facilitator, individuals can negotiate within a range of compensation packages that offer a wider array of risk and return.

Q: Are there problems with an SEU being too independent? In other words, isn't one of the benefits associated with an SEU the ability to bring entrepreneurial spirit back into the large company?

A: Yes. Although the large firm tends to exhibit too much control over small, local ventures, sometimes the opposite occurs when the large firm invests in a remote project. New high-potential ventures that are too far away may be completely ignored. General Motors and Toyota provide a useful example. In the 1980s, General Motors and Toyota formed a joint venture called "Neumi." This venture was designed as an attempt to produce a small vehicle in the United States.

This joint venture also provided a learning lab and experimental organization for GM to clone or copy Japanese manufacturing and engineering techniques. The venture successfully produced vehicles branded as both Toyotas and Chevrolets. They sold moderately well, although the Toyota version always outsold the Chevy. The secondary objective, which was to provide a learning experience for General Motors executives, has generally been viewed (both internally and externally) as a failure. What happened here?

Groups of GM managers were trotted out to California to witness the Japanese methods and to see, first hand, how their process worked in an interrogated fashion. The plant was on the "must-tour" routine for all up-and-coming GM executives. Several were rotated into the plant management structure for one- or two-year assignments. But this behavior was all superficial to the core organization of GM. Back in Detroit, the not-invented-here syndrome took precedence. The strong-minded, arrogant U.S. automotive industry took control and locked out the valuable input that the joint venture could have provided.

Most departments within GM either refused to adopt the venture examples or found reasons to justify why this experiment would not work within the larger firm. Although the venture did lead to other joint research vehicles, GM decided to start from scratch in the establishment of its Saturn Division and basically duplicated rather than adopted the advantages that they could have learned from the Toyota venture. They spent considerably more money than was necessary, in part because the experiment was too far removed from the corporate buy-in (i.e., informal and formal network) necessary to make it succeed.

Q: Who should decide when to harvest, and when is the right time?

A: Outside financiers often make the harvest decision at a price and time that is convenient for them. This may not be in the best interest of other members of the SEU and parent firm. An outsider may not be interested in the long-term benefit of the deal or strategic investment and may only be interested in maximizing his or her gain in the short term. Large organizations, particularly those with publicly held stock, should not allow outsiders to drive this important decision. Large, publicly traded organizations can provide investor liquidity through a swap with existing stock, if necessary. When it comes to deal structure and harvest, the venture should only be harvested (i.e., sold or made into IPO) when it appears that an important funding or strategic link is necessary to maximize value. This step should be made clear at venture formation along with the company objective. To add or change the harvest later, once success or failure appears evident, becomes expensive in either respect.

Q: What should be the primary purpose of forming the new SEU venture?

A: Before beginning the venture process, senior management needs to decide what they hope to accomplish. There may be at least five different reasons why management would like to pursue growth through ventures including: (1) strategic expansion of the firm into new areas, (2) technological acquisition, (3) new product development, (4) new market entry, and (5) cultural change. Depending on the purpose, the structure of the facility will *obviously vary.*

Q: Who should run the new SEU venture and where do the entrepreneurs come from?

A: The answer to this question varies with the level of expertise and staffing within the organization. Ideally, talented entrepreneurs converge from both the inside and outside. However, in the past some organizations experimented with "think-tanks" and "skunk-works" projects in which senior managers self-selected "entrepreneurial" people and placed them in entrepreneurial units (perhaps even physically separated from the main operations). These projects often failed because the experiments did not simulate real, entrepreneurial environment conditions.

Often, wealth creation develops with small homogeneous populations sharing a common culture and ideology. Bringing in people with a diverse background or mindset may be detrimental to deal formation. If the organization forces certain members into a team that it deems necessary, it may seriously disrupt or impede the development of the operation. This may hold true irrespective of the educational base or skill set of the added member. In a perfect world, the team will be self-generating and highly motivated to excel at its chosen task. Our early research efforts in this regard suggest that small groups with similar values (work ethic, motivations, goals, etc.) work best in creating successful ventures. Large organizations need to be careful not to meddle in these sensitive value-creating dynamics.

Q: How can large companies change their middle managers and unmotivated employees into entrepreneurs?

A: They can't. A lazy employee will probably not turn into a dynamic EntrePartneur. Although it would be nice to extract value from this large middle group, most middle managers have little incentive to pursue any risk initiative. Moreover, they are not willing to risk their compensation and will probably resent those around them that receive unusual rewards or recognition while betting their corporate assets and future livelihood. The SEU approach applies a compensation-based methodology that engages individuals (inside and external to the organization) to pursue entrepreneurial paths. Given the self-selection bias that may exist at large organizations (i.e., individuals willing to engage in risk/ return may not be willing to work for a large company), it may be likely that the organization will need to search outside the organization for entrepreneurs.

Where possible, the goal should be to encourage middle managers to be supportive of entrepreneurial activities in the work environment (or at the very least be neutral toward venture creation) and not to impede the progress of the entrepreneurial members within. The middle managers

should see any of their contributions, even minor support
(i.e., idea development or product outlets), rewarded with
recognition, compensation (bonus, etc.), or both.

Q: Should large companies turn entrepreneurs into employees?

A: No. During the mid- to late-1990s, so-called rollups, leverage buildups and consolidations were all the rage on Wall
Street. Many companies were quick to buy out entrepreneurs and place them on a graduated earn out clause (3–5
years). The intent was to get them out of the business as
soon as possible so that management could continue with its
cost reductions and corporate consolidations. In quick fashion, some organizations turned highly productive entrepreneurs into drones within the organization. Indications of
what the organization had done could be observed in the
types of questions asked by the bought-out entrepreneurs.[1]
"How many weeks vacation can I take?", "Can I leave early
for my son's (daughter's) baseball (soccer) game?", "What
are the minimum number of hours I have to work per
week?" The companies usually didn't do anything specific to
drive these questions, but clearly individuals who were
accustomed to calling all of the shots themselves were now
thinking like an employee. Their focus shifted immediately
from increasing the business to working the minimum effort.
This is the exact opposite of what large companies need.
They need to change employees into entrepreneurs. Sadly,
their experience traditionally has been to do the opposite. If
they are to be successful in growing organically, they need to
create incentive systems to reverse this long trend. Otherwise, the declining pattern will only continue.

---

1. During the mid-1990s, we surveyed over 40 prospective "roll-up" or consolidation
   candidates in the medical industry. These were individuals whose companies were
   being pursued in a friendly acquisition with the purpose of "rolling up" many in
   the same industry and then taking the entire group public through an IPO. The
   comments included in the text are consistent with the general tone of the group.

Q: Who should help negotiate the terms of the new venture creations?

A: Large companies should attempt to hire an unbiased individual/group to negotiate internal and external deals. Often a large company may try to negotiate the deals directly, primarily because they want to control the process and use their considerable leverage to negotiate the best terms. However, it is our contention that because the negotiations are so one-sided and predictable, many internal entrepreneurs choose not to negotiate at all. In fact, they may prefer to either (1) withhold promising ventures reserving the right to exercise these ideas later or (2) leave the organization to set up a new venture on their own. In either situation, the large organization loses. Furthermore, to the extent that many ideas may expire or become stale due to advancements in the marketplace or obsolescence, there may be considerable "untapped value" within the organization that could be easily extracted. The external negotiators should be reasonable and impartial. Moreover, both the large organization and the entrepreneurial team should pay the negotiator to remove the perception of bias. The large company might be able to draft a short list of potential negotiators, and then after an interview process, the entrepreneurial team could select from that list. Thus, both parties will be responsible and comfortable with this important member of the deal formation and development.

Q: Should large companies seek a large corporate law firm to handle all of the negotiations and intellectual property negotiation issues?

A: No. We do not advocate the use of large corporate law firms for handling the negotiation or ombudsman process. Although the knowledge of lawyers will be very helpful at defining parameters related to IP issues, unfortunately, in many situations lawyers have an economic disincentive to be efficient and may have no limit to billings on an hourly basis. Moreover, given their strong leverage against their client, they can develop a coherent argument or series of arguments to justify their wages making it more difficult for the parent company to limit the size or scope of their legal work. It usually follows the line of protectionism for the big company and may be difficult to disengage (i.e., without them the company will lose valuable rights or be vulnerable to large payoffs down the road). Law firms should be helpful in setting up the initial parameters of the SEU and intellectual property rights and responsibilities, but should not be placed in control as the SEU Facilitator.

The last thing the large company wants or needs is the loss of their organizational lifeblood. However, when it comes to negotiations with small entrepreneurs, a large corporate legal staff may be unnecessary or wasteful. Large companies need to be more efficient in employing their legal protection. In some cases, such as Microsoft's case against the U.S. Justice department, there is no alternative. There is no negotiation. There is no compromise. The large company needs to take the offensive and fight for its stakeholder rights and privileges. However, there are plenty of situations, indeed perhaps most, in which the company is not fighting for its constitutional rights. In these cases it needs to be practical. It needs to be efficient. It needs to be forward-looking in its application and purpose. In these situations the company needs to address the benefits to all parties and think about how it can best grow the firm through mutual cooperation. The corporate lawyers need to step aside. They may be too biased to represent the firm efficiently in these situations.

Q: What is the primary role of the third-party Facilitator?

A: The Facilitator should represent all parties to the deal in a fair and proper manner. This means that the Facilitator sets as a stated priority or objective to first protect the interests of the "SEU" and not just the rights of the large organization. The Facilitator should help develop a simple template offering rights and privileges to all stakeholders in the deal. So long as the interests of the "SEU deal" are represented first and foremost, the direction ought to be clear. This is an important first step to developing strategic growth through entrepreneurial partners (e.g., "EntrePartneurs"). It will be a contentious first step hotly debated within the inner circle. Ultimately, many companies will not relax control and will not follow through with this recommendation. This is to be expected. The organization will at first need to select a catalyst or corporate champion to lead the charge, but once the infrastructure has been established, it should no longer depend on that corporate champion's energies alone. Otherwise, the facility may not survive an economic downturn or change in organizational leadership, and may risk losing the opportunity for long-term value creation.

Q: *Should large companies continue to focus on employee stock option plans to generate employee alignment with shareholder interests?*

A: No, we do not believe that large companies should focus on general stock option plans. The vast majority of individuals do not have influence on the overall stock price and usually do not have enough stock options to make a substantive difference in their behavior. However, we do advocate the creation of new economic incentive packages allowing for "pure play" or venture-specific opportunities. Large companies need to reduce stock option plays on total firm and increase option plays for new venture appreciation or growth within the large company. Some employees need and should be able to develop an equity stake or accumulated equity interest in a long-term venture. Because the efforts of most employees have little, if any, effect on the large company, arguably the best way to provide employees with a meaningful ownership interest would be to provide a stake within a smaller venture. This would improve their vested interest over an extended time period and increase the likelihood that they would seek to enhance venture revenues and reduce venture costs. Moreover, providing equity in a smaller venture would increase the accountability and linkage between the individual's efforts and the development of true value.

Executives of a large company need to make big changes to the company to influence the stock. Otherwise, their stock options won't have much value. As we've seen with the M&A activity of the 1990s, significant transaction activity is not in the best interests of all stakeholders. Large company stock options only make sense for a few individuals, and even here, it is not clear whether the incentives are always aligned properly. If individuals in the executive circle only have a few years to see their job through, they are under immediate pressure to accelerate performance quickly. Whether or not it is in the long-term best interests of all parties may be secondary to their mission. Irrespective of their urgency to change, they have economic incentive to search for the "quick fix." If the stock market reacts favorably during their tenure, they are afforded a rare treat and perhaps favorable popular press clippings. Their stock options are tied to the total performance of the organization. They may be able to change the development and general movement of the organization. But overnight, they cannot change the organic profit equation. This takes time and strategic focus.

Q: *In negotiations, why shouldn't large companies attempt to maximize their economic stake and attempt to own 100% of the equity in any new venture creation?*

A: Given their enormous resources and leverage, large companies can exert heavy-handed negotiations and demand a large percentage of any new business ventures with their internal candidates. However, this will reduce entrepreneurial incentive and reduce the likelihood that others will attempt to maximize the economic value and growth of the new initiative. Moreover, by consistently taking 100% of the equity, large companies may be providing incentive for entrepreneurial employees to leave the organization (where employees can earn equity on their own). If organizations want to facilitate new growth in a dynamic new manner, they will need to become accustomed to giving up part of the upside. Otherwise they may continue to own everything in ventures with little or no potential.

Q: Should large companies license or sell their IP?

A: Wherever possible it is best to continue an ownership stake in the intellectual property. This becomes particularly important with intellectual property of a strategic interest. Most large firms refuse to sell or license their intellectual property out of concern for its control and misuse. On the other hand, some companies, particularly during periods of economic recession, may be inclined to sell intellectual property to generate cash. Given the timing of the sale and the poor negotiating position of the selling firm, the revenue may not be maximized in this way. As an alternative, we believe the firm should consider more licensing arrangements that provide economic incentive for outsiders to promote its products. As the brand recognition improves, the large company will find that it is growing faster with no incremental investment.

Q: What is the best way to respond to Wall Street criticisms?

A: Wall Street analysts tend to be focused on corporate revenue and profit growth. Moreover, they tend to be keenly interested in their own compensation and incentive systems that may or may not correspond with the long-term best interests of the large firm's stakeholders. So long as the large firm is focused on new product innovations and new methodologies to enhance organic growth and keep administrative costs low, Wall Street will be unable to find fault with management practice. Moreover, as the organization becomes increasingly transparent in its growth methodologies and compensation mechanisms, fewer surprises and potential improprieties will likely occur, thus reducing the potential volatility of the company's stock price.

Management needs to be careful not to fall prey to external consultants, dealmakers, lawyers, shareholders, suppliers, internal executives/managers, and other stakeholders who may all have varying economic incentives. Ultimately, it will probably not be possible to satisfy the interests of all stakeholders and potential stakeholder groups. However, management needs to balance the interests of each party and select the path that maximizes stakeholder welfare. Ultimately, creating a venture with true organic growth helps expand the economic pie for the mutual benefit of all stakeholders.

Q: *Should organizations create an environment that provides a long-term lock-up of key talent?*

A: Creating an environment that discourages talent flight may only serve to make employees increasingly dependent and resentful of the parent firm. Organizations need to think of ways to partner with some value-creating employees that will reduce the organizational cost structure and allow members to work with the firm on an independent basis. This may increase the flexibility to source with multiple agents and allow the entrepreneur to allocate cost structure to multiple parties (separate from the parent firm). However, organizations need to be careful that their new venturing facilities do not create incentive for the valuable employees to leave while the less mobile (and less valuable) individuals remain.

Q: *Can new ventures actually create growth with no incremental overhead?*

A: Yes. By licensing and partnering with former employees or external parties, large companies might be able to increase their revenues and profits without any additional investment capital or management oversight. Once management creates a basic template that invites external and internal participation, it theoretically should be able to appreciably enhance its shareholders' return on investment (ROI) due to the lack of incremental investment. The implementation of this approach mandates that the company not over-invest or over-manage these new areas. This would require relaxing traditional areas of control or domination that may be difficult in practice to implement. However, the theoretical model should be held as a benchmark in which to judge future performance (i.e., measure administrative overhead).

Q: *Isn't it a mathematical certainty that in order for a large company to engage in any detectable growth, it needs to grow through large projects? Why should management even care about small, organizational growth?*

A: It is true that large companies need considerable growth to make any meaningful difference to the investor community. However, we disagree that it needs to come from large investments. In fact, the empirical evidence over the past decade makes increasingly clear that growth through large acquisitions or purchases may be the fastest way to lose value for corporate stakeholders. We advocate value creation or partnering with many smaller, high-growth entrepreneurial units. Although the contributions from any single source may be insignificant, we believe that in the aggregate a portfolio of these entities can provide appreciable growth and a substantive, measurable difference to the corporate bottom line.

Q: *Why do you believe that growth should occur through smaller entrepreneurial units? Why not take advantage of the economies of scale attributed to the large firm?*

A: In theory, large firms offer extraordinary economies of scale. They have resources only dreamed about by small entrepreneurial firms: talent, capital, brand, distribution, and so forth. However, despite these enormous advantages, large firms are just too inefficient to manage their resources in a productive manner. We believe large companies should provide a vehicle of growth for small companies. Given their ability to lend specific expertise, cheap capital, brand, and distribution, large companies can bring value added to the bargaining table, but then they need to step aside. Small companies provide accountability for their employees and management team and will not squander their scarce resources. Moreover, the small entrepreneurial venture will more likely figure out a way to make things work, even if at first pass, it appears that there are difficult barriers in the way. Entrepreneurs learn how to manage risks and motivate their key people. They can be more responsive to market conditions and adapt faster than the large firm to the mutual benefit of all of their stakeholders.

Q: *Why do large firms eventually die?*

A: Interestingly enough, our study suggests that the median age of the *Fortune 500* company is about 54 years. Although some may last longer than 200 years, that is clearly the exception to the rule. We believe that as organizations age it becomes increasingly difficult for all stakeholders to maintain the same motivating goal. Although a few events may galvanize the organizational viewpoint, such as a public stock offering or a strategic sale, acquisition, or merger, for the most part, individuals pursue an individual path that may come at the expense of most other stakeholders. Collectively, these individual paths may not necessarily benefit other members of the firm to the ultimate detriment of all other stakeholders.

Where possible, the firm should attempt to create accountability and growth through separate operating units. For example, although Johnson and Johnson is over 116 years old, it provides a shining example of how some old companies can maintain an aggressive growth pattern. In the last 10 to 20 years it seems to have gotten even more profitable and maintains more than 200 separate operating units. We believe it may be possible for other firms to replicate this pattern of growth or more through separate, albeit related, operating units. We also believe that it is beneficial to provide equity incentive to participants, where possible.

Q: *How can large companies reduce their cost structure and increase their focus?*

A: Organizations that scale back from their non-strategic initiatives can reduce their cost structure and improve their ROI. The improvement in ROI results from SEU formations or facilities in which individuals embrace risk (their own capital and time) for mutual gain. This enables management to free up their time to focus on strategic issues and direction, without losing sight of the larger prizes and future growth.

Q: What are the most compelling reason(s) to embrace an SEU concept?

A: The SEU concept essentially enables the large company to bet on people who are betting on themselves. On an individual basis, many of these people may not be able to generate a strong company alone. However, the large company should hold a portfolio of SEU investments. On net, these SEUs will make a fine, perhaps even outstanding, investment. Remember, the individual entrepreneurs in an SEU do not have a backup plan. They are investing their own capital and career path, as well as the livelihood of their dependents, on the success of their new venture. They do not want to fail. Indeed, many of them will operate as if they *can't* fail. From a portfolio perspective, the large firm may not be able to perform better than betting on this group that quite literally may be betting everything on themselves.

Q: What are the key attributes of a new business facility?

A: The concept should be simple in design with an easy entry and exit feature. If it is too complex or cumbersome, it may frighten away potentially good investments and people. Moreover, the project should be fluid, flexible, and fair enough to address unanticipated problems without undue stress or controversy to participants in the venture. The ideal SEU facility will provide equity participation and fair compensation to the value creators. It will have relatively little administrative overhead and day-to-day monitoring and mutual trust developed over time. Moreover, the group must have a common sense of purpose and destination. If goal alignment does not exist among the key stakeholders, it may be become problematic later on as stakeholders age and goals diverge.

Q: How does the SEU venture leverage the firm's R & D?

A: By creating an opportunity to partner with entrepreneurial individuals, both internal and external to the organization, the large firm can amplify its return on investment and leverage its research and development. Although new projects will tend to be extensions of company brand and distribution channels they can really develop in a number of ways.

Clever entrepreneurs (both internal and external to the organization) will examine methods in which they can combine their talents, expertise and intellectual property with the large firm to create a product or service that is mutually beneficial. This means that the large company will be able to extend its set of opportunities without incremental investment. In effect, it will be leveraging its existing investment in research and development in a very efficient manner.

Q: *If applied appropriately, will an SEU require more or less risk capital investment by the firm compared to traditional corporate venturing?*

A: Since the SEU approach combines the brand and intellectual property of the large firm with the intellectual property of the entrepreneur, it should require less risk capital investment by the large firm. Rather than making a direct capital investment in another strategic area or acquisition, the large firm can simply partner with entrepreneurs and allow each to earn an equity-like return on whichever aspect each brings to the negotiating table. There is no need for the large firm to invest in areas which may consume capital with a low or negative return. The firm will be able to simply broker deals (and contribute no capital) and license its brand, distribution capabilities, patents or other intellectual property. This will enable the firm to essentially earn an unlimited return on investment (ROI) as the incremental revenue will accrue with no incremental investment. Of course, given the size of most large, public companies it may require a number of small SEU investments to make a significant contribution to the overall bottom line.

Q: *Given the size of most large, publicly-traded companies, and the small size of the SEU ventures, why should senior management consider these tiny, insignificant projects? Shouldn't management focus its energies on the strategic projects/ investments that will make a difference to the future of the organization and to its shareholders?*

A: Growing a multibillion dollar organization through a series of small $0.5 to $2 million projects will be a logistical and administrative challenge. However, the SEU template does not encourage senior management to spend its valuable time structuring, negotiating and nurturing small entrepreneurial ventures. Rather, management should set up an external growth initiative program and select an independent (unbiased) Facilitator that will help solicit, review and approve appropriate deals. Given the modest or non-existent investment requirements of many deals (e.g., licensing intellectual property or distribution channels), the SEUs can only help to serve the demands of the investment community and other corporate stakeholders. Meanwhile, management can still pursue its large scale strategic investments. The process is not mutually exclusive. In fact, given the tendency of large companies to make a few, closely-monitored large strategic bets (in order to have an impact on the bottom line) the SEU approach provides a buffer from a portfolio perspective. In the unfortunate event that management makes a large strategic bet that fails (e.g., Motorola's $1 billion + investment in satellite technology--Iridium), the company can still fall back on its diversified investment base of SEU projects. Thus, an SEU program can only serve to reinforce an overall growth strategy.

Q: *Can this new model work in privately held organizations or in the governmental sector?*

A: Yes. Although our work has been based on data collected primarily, but not exclusively, from large, publicly traded organizations, we are now seeing evidence that nonprofit entities such as Battelle are employing an SEU-type venture. Many of the same problems addressing large, publicly held companies also exist in large privately held companies and governmental agencies. These include divergent goals, poor compensation mechanisms, and aversion to risk. Both privately held companies and governmental agencies have unique attributes that make them different from our primary sample of publicly held companies. In some cases, there are characteristics that make them live longer (governmental agencies with long-term commitment and funding). Or, there are some attributes that might make them operate more efficiently (privately held companies with founder/owner focus and control). Further studies will research these different groups and attempt to offer insights about mechanisms that will enable them to grow faster or more efficiently. To the extent that some lessons might apply the other way, perhaps we will see future companies less likely to pursue an IPO, or more companies opting to privatize. We do not know yet what future data will uncover. We do believe, however, that future modifications will continue to apply to other sectors, possibly with far-reaching ramifications.

Q: *Assuming that a large company is interested in pursuing a new model of growth, when is the best time to implement these plans?*

A: Now! The risk of continuing on the same path may be greater than the risk of undertaking new twists to older models of growth. Certainly the answer is not to remain constant. Doing nothing is virtually guaranteeing failure. Organizations have pursued many models of growth in the past 30 years. Most of the quick answers don't work, though some offer valuable enhancements to long-term wealth creation.

Perhaps the clearest danger to the large firm is in the administration of this new model. It is designed as a "low administrative" approach. Creating hierarchy and layers of management is the surest way to kill this method. The large company needs a high-level company champion to help establish the new facility and then get out of the way. If the facility is set up with the proper incentives then it will drive itself. It does not require, nor advocate, heavy-handed oversight or day-to-day administration by the corporate office.

When resources are low, such as during an economic recession, the SEU approach could not be better timed. It should be implemented without delay. If large companies ever expect to grow bigger, they will need to learn how to grow through smaller companies. Given their recent history they should not postpone this path. They need to begin today.

Q: Can you identify any companies that have currently experimented with an SEU template? If not, are there any companies that come close?

A: Yes! In 2003 Battelle started to experiment with a model that is extremely close to an SEU template. In a strategic relationship with Babson College, Battelle has explored new entrepreneurial initiatives in an attempt to develop its extensive R&D intellectual property. Babson College is essentially acting as an unbiased SEU "Facilitator" by filtering deal flow, selecting prospective entrepreneurial employees (from its student population), facilitating the development of the budding enterprises, and assisting with negotiations. Because this initiative is now in its early stages, no progress report is yet available. However, early "deal flows" thus far have concentrated on simple licensing arrangements and distribution channels.

Microsoft's XBox venture also comes close to an SEU template. Although specific terms of the XBox deal are not available, much public information regarding this venture suggests that it was set up with an "SEU-type flavor." Entrepreneurial employees (e.g., EntrePartneurs) appear to have equity rights along with the corporate parent. Moreover, the funding and development of intellectual property along with the operational independence and extraordinary arbiter or mediator to the deal (Bill Gates) suggests that many of the SEU concepts are represented in this venture arrangement. Given the embracing of talent external to the organization, it actually represents what we refer to as a "reverse SEU" in which the entrepreneurs come from outside the organization and form a deal.

Many other large companies may already be offering some version of the SEU template, though not on a consistent, company-wide basis. In these situations, companies may set up new ventures on a case-by-case basis with senior management providing the deal flow and filtering. For example, Ford Motor Company has structured minority-owned strategic ventures with former employees and other third-party participants (e.g., "EntrePartneurs") on a limited basis.

Finally, companies such as Johnson and Johnson have a more distant formation, though it also approaches an SEU template. Johnson and Johnson, for example, encourages the formation of many separate divisions and operating entities within its large and diverse organization. Many of these are located near their New Jersey Corporate offices for logistical and coordination reasons. Others are located completely across the country where talent and unique markets reside or where it is easier to retain independence from other corporate groups. It depends on the product and where the company is in its initial startup curve. However, each division receives economic incentive for superior performance and appears to operate with little corporate interference. Furthermore, for a relatively old, large, publicly traded company, it appears to continue with relatively strong revenue and profit performance.

Conclusion

Management of large companies needs to be sensitive to their investments and constantly be seeking ways to maximize future output and minimize costs irrespective of internal politics or external market dynamics. Otherwise, the organization is doomed to develop in ways that may not be productive. Entrepreneurial behavior focuses on growth and new venture creation. Entrepreneurs hold true to principles of value generation despite corporate bureaucracy, inefficiency, and waste. Companies and economic environments that stay focused to these guiding principles will prosper at the expense of those who don't. The early 2000s have been a tough economic time period for all participants, but entrepreneurial behavior continues. Survivors through the next cycle must learn the important lessons of frugality and wealth creation or suffer the consequences. Many large companies may not survive, although there still may be opportunity to grow.

We believe entrepreneurial talent exists and is productive irrespective of difficult economic conditions. Further, we believe that true entrepreneurial behavior operates best in small clusters without extensive corporate governance or bureaucratic interference. Although large corporations may be terrific at generating large-scale, heavy R&D technologies, many tend not to be efficient with capital resources or financial management. Large companies need to learn these important lessons before it's too late. Otherwise, they'll be forced to operate as a small business that was once a big business (like Lucent, moving from 135,000 employees to 30,000 employees).

Small, entrepreneurial ventures are more efficient than large companies and likely to continue with product innovations at the same time that large companies scale back. They learn how to grow whether they currently have the talent or whether they make the conditions ripe for talent to work with them. They are savvy and know how to compete with few resources. These are attributes uncommon within many large organizations. This means, more than ever, that large firms need small firms to help them grow. Large firms have the economic resources to stay alive longer than small firms, but often do not have the organizational mindset that best manages their day-to-day operations. Thus, if the large firm really wants entrepreneurial behavior and growth, we advocate that they behave like a small firm.

We believe the implementation of an SEU, although not appropriate for all firms, is a step in the right direction for many. Further, we believe that a move toward entrepreneurial spirit and compensation works in the best interests of most stakeholders in the long term. But organizational bureaucracy and economic disincentives will make implementation difficult. However, some brave CEOs will venture forward and attempt a new twist to prior venture models. For many large, public organizations, growth is not coming close to its potential and the company is not capitalizing on its intellectual property and expertise. Through the 1970s, 1980s, and 1990s, many corporate venturing experiments have been presented with varying levels of success. The SEU template offers a modification to the best features of these old models. Large organizations can get bigger but they will need to grow in smaller units. Collectively, these smaller, high-growth ventures will contribute to a more prosperous, entrepreneurial organization.

INDEX

8 reasons why you should read the Financial Times for 4 weeks RISK-FREE!

To help you stay current with significant
developments in the world economy ...
and to assist you to make informed business
decisions — the Financial Times brings you:

❶ Fast, meaningful overviews of international affairs ... plus daily
briefings on major world news.

❷ Perceptive coverage of economic, business, financial and political
developments with special focus on emerging markets.

❸ More international business news than any other publication.

❹ Sophisticated financial analysis and commentary on world market
activity plus stock quotes from over 30 countries.

❺ Reports on international companies and a section on global investing.

❻ Specialized pages on management, marketing, advertising and
technological innovations from all parts of the world.

❼ Highly valued single-topic special reports (over 200 annually)
on countries, industries, investment opportunities, technology and more.

❽ The Saturday Weekend FT section — a globetrotter's guide to
leisure-time activities around the world: the arts, fine dining, travel,
sports and more.

FT FINANCIAL TIMES
World business newspaper

The *Financial Times* delivers a world of business news.

Use the Risk-Free Trial Voucher below!

To stay ahead in today's business world you need to be well-informed on a daily basis. And not just on the national level. You need a news source that closely monitors the entire world of business, and then delivers it in a concise, quick-read format.

With the *Financial Times* you get the major stories from every region of the world. Reports found nowhere else. You get business, management, politics, economics, technology and more.

Now you can try the *Financial Times* for 4 weeks, absolutely risk free. And better yet, if you wish to continue receiving the *Financial Times* you'll get great savings off the regular subscription rate. Just use the voucher below.

---

4 Week Risk-Free Trial Voucher

Yes! Please send me the *Financial Times* for 4 weeks (Monday through Saturday) Risk-Free, and details of special subscription rates in my country.

Name _____

Company _____

Address _____ ❑ Business or ❑ Home Address

Apt./Suite/Floor _____ City _____ State/Province _____

Zip/Postal Code _____ Country _____

Phone (optional) _____ E-mail (optional) _____

Limited time offer good for new subscribers in FT delivery areas only.

To order contact Financial Times Customer Service in your area (mention offer SAB01A).

The Americas: Tel 800-628-8088 Fax 845-566-8220 E-mail: uscirculation@ft.com

Europe: Tel 44 20 7873 4200 Fax 44 20 7873 3428 E-mail: fte.subs@ft.com

Japan: Tel 0120 341-468 Fax 0120 593-146 E-mail: circulation.fttokyo@ft.com

Korea: E-mail: sungho.yang@ft.com

S.E. Asia: Tel 852 2905 5555 Fax 852 2905 5590 E-mail: subseasia@ft.com

www.ft.com

FT FINANCIAL TIMES
World business newspaper

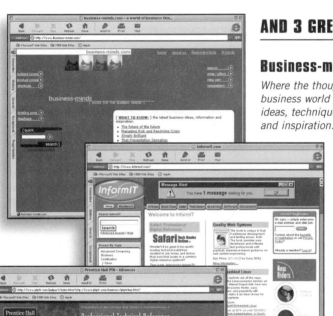